P9-CEH-044

GAY
America
STRUGGLE FOR EQUALITY

Linas Alsenas

AMULET BOOKS ★ NEW YORK

9/10/10

Acknowledgments
In addition to the many people who have assisted his research, reviewed this text, and offered invaluable advice, the author would like to extend special thanks to Suzanne Harper, Maggie Lehrman, Katelyn Lahr, Maria Middleton, Scott Auerbach, Susan Van Metre, Tamar Brazis, Jason Wells, Jan Wilhelmsson, and particularly Howard Reeves, without whom this book would simply not exist.

FOR HOWARD

* * * * *

TITLE PAGE: Keith Haring painting *Crack Is Wack* mural, 1986. Haring was an artist working in the 1980s who often used his work to generate activism and awareness about AIDS.

Library of Congress Cataloging-in-Publication Data
Alsenas, Linas.
Gay America : struggle for equality / Linas Alsenas.
p. cm.
ISBN-13: 978-0-8109-9487-4
ISBN-10: 0-8109-9487-9
1. Gays—United States—History. 2. Gay rights—United States—History. 3. Gay liberation movement—United States—History. I. Title.

HQ76.3.U5A37 2008
306.76'60973—dc22
2007028066

Text copyright © 2008 Linas Alsenas
For illustration credits please see page 156

Book design by Maria T. Middleton

Published in 2008 by Amulet Books,
an imprint of Harry N. Abrams, Inc.

All rights reserved. No portion of this book may be reproduced, stored in a retrieval system, or transmitted in any form or by any means, mechanical, electronic, photocopying, recording, or otherwise, without written permission from the publisher.

Printed and bound in China
10 9 8 7 6 5 4 3 2 1

HNA
harry n. abrams, inc.
a subsidiary of La Martinière Groupe
115 West 18th Street
New York, NY 10011
www.hnabooks.com

CONTENTS

The original rainbow flag, designed by San Francisco artist Gilbert Baker, has been a symbol of gay and lesbian pride since its introduction in 1978. Initially it had eight stripes but was later pared down to six.

FOREWORD

GAYS AND LESBIANS play a very prominent role in American life today, whether grabbing headlines over political gains, starring in and being the subject of movies and television shows, or filling the streets of nearly every major city to celebrate Gay Pride every year. Cities and city districts such as Northampton and Provincetown in Massachusetts, Chelsea and Park Slope in New York City, the Castro and Bernal Heights in San Francisco, West Hollywood in Los Angeles, and Boys Town in Chicago are known for their thriving queer communities, while gay-oriented businesses from cruise ships to cable networks flourish.

Moreover, there exists a blossoming field of academic scholarship on the subjects of gay and lesbian history and identity, queer politics, and gender theory. This book is an attempt to open up that historical scholarly activity to teens who arguably need access to it the most.

Studying the history of gay and lesbian people can be a very slippery business. Just as with heterosexuals, lesbians and gays are hard to define in any age, and grouping them together across time adds further complications. I include figures and events that have been claimed by queer men and women in reconstructing the history of their community beginning with the Victorian era—because it was during that time the word "homosexual" appeared in America to describe a kind of person, an identity.

The history of homosexuality in America is *huge*—and it grows more complex every day. This book could not possibly claim to be a complete history. Instead, the events and people discussed in this book were chosen to create an entertaining narrative that readers could use as a foothold as they begin to learn about the rich heritage of gay and lesbian life in America. My narrative tries to focus on the most dramatic, trailbreaking moments and personalities, and it omits the everyday struggles and joys of the millions of gays and lesbians who lived unrecorded lives with silent courage throughout the period. It is important to note that there often are exceptions to every rule—what is happening in New York may not be true in Oakland, California, for example, or the experience of one racial or ethnic group may differ vastly from the experience of others. A broad narrative such as this must inevitably make wide statements that are open (rightly!) to question. Since space is limited, I have focused on the histories of gays and lesbians, leaving out many of the histories of the increasingly diverse groups within the queer community whose stories are tightly woven into the same historical fabric. I have also avoided discussion of the scientific arguments about the origins and functions of same-sex attraction.

My historical retelling is entirely indebted to the work of many dedicated archivists, journalists, and historians, most notably Paula Gunn Allen, Brett Beemyn, Allan Bérubé, Nan Alamilla Boyd, George Chauncey, Dudley Clendinen and Adam Nagourney, Blanche Weisen Cook, John D'Emilio, Allen Drexel, Martin Duberman, Lisa Duggan, Lillian Faderman, Marcia M. Gallo, Eric Garber, Kevin Jennings, David K. Johnson, Elizabeth Lapovsky Kennedy and Madeline D. Davis, Charles Kaiser, Jonathan Ned Katz, Eric Marcus, Beatrice Medicine, Neil Miller, Leila J. Rupp, Randy Shilts, Roey Thorpe, and Walter Williams.

Each part of this book is introduced with a story told from a personalized point of view; while each of those stories is based on true accounts, they are my words. I hope the reader will take my subjectivity into account and that anyone who reads this book will have lots and lots of questions. I encourage her or him to dig deeper into the material by going to the resources listed in the endnotes and the bibliography.

"The 'Love that dare not speak its name' in this century . . . is that deep, spiritual affection that is as pure as it is perfect. . . . It is beautiful, it is fine, it is the noblest form of affection. There is nothing unnatural about it . . . . That it should be so the world does not understand. The world mocks at it and sometimes puts one in the pillory for it."

—OSCAR WILDE DURING HIS 1895 TRIAL FOR "GROSS INDECENCY"

 FRIENDS WITH BENEFITS
PRE-TWENTIETH CENTURY

Memphis, Tennessee, 1892

"ALICE," THE DOCTOR ASKED, "do you not know that you could not have married another young lady?" The very idea was preposterous—that alone could prove the girl was insane. But the idea did not seem ridiculous to the patient.

"Oh," she answered, "I could have married Freda."

The doctor stared intently at the girl. She *appeared* to be quite reasonable, despite her words. Indeed, Alice appeared to be like any other nineteen-year-old girl. She had large, close-set eyes that had an alert, intelligent gaze. She was thin, and her skin was rather sallow, but that seemed understandable under the circumstances: no one looks their best in jail.

The daughter of a well-to-do family, Alice had attended Miss Higbee's School for Young Ladies with Freda Ward, who was two years younger, and the two of them started "chumming" several years ago. They became passionate about each other—obsessive, really. Then, almost two years ago, Miss Ward's family moved away to Golddust, a small town eighty miles north on the Mississippi. Nevertheless, the pair continued their intense friendship with visits and absurdly romantic letters. Alice had even proposed that they elope, to which Miss Ward apparently agreed.

On second thought, the doctor considered, perhaps Alice's facial features *were* a bit asymmetrical and her forehead a bit low. It might be worth mentioning in court. Newspapers from San Francisco to New York had been covering this story, and Dr. B. F. Turner was well aware of what this case meant for his career. It was quite an honor that the defense hired such a young doctor as one of its experts.

"But someone usually has to support a family in a case like that," the doctor continued, bringing his thoughts back to the conversation.

"I know, and I was going to support both." Alice said it as if it were obvious.

Dr. Turner rubbed his chin thoughtfully. No, he decided, her face revealed nothing out of the ordinary. No one on the street would ever guess that the young lady seated before him was, in fact, a monster. Perhaps her mother really was to blame. Alice's father, a retired furniture merchant, had tearfully explained to Dr. Turner how his wife had been temporarily sent to a lunatic asylum for "puerperal insanity" after the birth of their first child, the first of seven. It was not unlikely that this girl had inherited her mother's sickness.

"But a girl like you could not earn enough for both," he pointed out.

"But I was going to dress as a man . . ." Alice faltered, and she blinked several times.

Clearly, this girl had a weak grasp on reality. Dr. Turner had heard of such cases, of women living their lives disguised as men, but he was sure those stories were the product of silly, sensationalized

A MOST SHOCKING CRIME

A MEMPHIS SOCIETY GIRL CUTS A FORMER FRIEND'S THROAT.

ALICE MITCHELL, DAUGHTER OF A WEALTHY RETIRED MERCHANT, JUMPS FROM A CARRIAGE, SEIZES FREDA WARD, AND KILLS HER.

MEMPHIS, Tenn., Jan. 25.—A sensational tragedy occurred here this afternoon. The victim was a young woman, and her slayer is of the same sex. Both were familiar figures in society. A few minutes before 4 o'clock a buggy containing Miss Alice Mitchell and Lizzie Johnston drove up to the broad sidewalk around the Custom House block leading to the levee. The lines were in the hands of Miss Johnston, and beside her, calm and self-possessed, sat Miss Mitchell.

Coming slowly up the steep incline from the river were Miss Freda Ward of Gold Dust, Ark., and her sister Jo, who had just put another sister, Mrs. Cummins, aboard the steamer Rosa Lee, for Gold Dust, Ark. The young women were soon opposite the carriage, chatting pleasantly and paying no attention to their surroundings. Suddenly from out the carriage came Miss Mitchell. Grasping Miss Ward by the neck, she drew a bright razor from out the folds of her dress and without a word drew it across the throat of her victim. Miss Ward sank to the pavement in an instant, the blood pouring in torrents from the severed jugular.

The murdered girl's sister, who had by this time recovered from her astonishment, grappled with the woman and tried to hold her, but in a twinkling she, too, received a cut, but luckily only a trifling one, near the ear.

Miss Mitchell, being freed from Miss Ward, jumped into the buggy in an instant, and with the exclamation "Drive on, I've done it!" seized the whip and with Miss Johnson still holding the lines the pair were soon around the corner into Madison Street and away from the scene of the tragedy.

Miss Ward was picked up tenderly by the gathering crowd and a passing carriage was pressed into service, which conveyed her to the Rogers Infirmary. She was, however, beyond human aid, and expired just as the infirmary was reached. The body was then taken to an undertaking establishment.

At 6 o'clock this evening Chief of Police Davis arrested Miss Mitchell, who was found at her home on Union Street. She was conveyed to the jail in a carriage.

The cause of the crime is to-night not positively known, as Miss Mitchell refuses to say a word to anybody on the subject. It is said, however, that Miss Ward, who was visiting in this city, had, on former trips to Memphis, been the guest of Miss Mitchell. Lately she refused to partake of the hospitality of the Mitchell household, and refused, also, to recognize Miss Mitchell on the street. It is alleged that Miss Ward had made remarks of an uncomplimentary nature regarding Miss Mitchell, and this is supposed to have been the cause of the tragedy.

Miss Mitchell is the nineteen-year-old daughter of George Mitchell, a retired furniture dealer, and she and Miss Johnston, in the latter's stylish turn-out, were a familiar sight on the drives about the city. Miss Ward is the daughter of John Ward, a planter and wealthy merchant of Gold Dust, Ark. At the inquest this evening the jury rendered a verdict charging Miss Mitchell with premeditated murder.

To-night the murderess made a singular statement. It was that she loved Freda desperately, better than any one in the world; that she could not live without her, and that long ago they made a compact that if they should ever be separated they should kill each other. When she found that Josie had forbidden Freda to speak to her, she knew of nothing else to do but to kill her. The girl is regarded as demented. The deceased was seventeen, and the murderess is only nineteen years old.

journalism. With a mind as unsteady as Alice's, such bizarre notions could have taken a terrible hold.

"But Miss Mitchell, do you not know that usually when young people get married, they look forward to the time when they shall have children growing up around them?" Miss Ward's older sister had found out and put a stop to the girls' elopement plans—she forced Freda to return Alice's engagement ring last summer and insisted they cut off contact.

"Oh, yes, sir."

But now poor Freda Ward would never have the opportunity to marry a man and bear children: she was lying in a coffin in Elmwood Cemetery.

Driving her buggy with a friend through town one chilly Monday afternoon in January, Alice Mitchell had spotted Freda walking with her sister and a friend. Alice slowed the buggy and followed the girls down to the boat landing. She stopped the carriage, jumped down, and hurried to catch up. At the tracks, Alice grabbed Freda Ward and slit her throat wide open with her father's shaving razor. She had been carrying the razor around for two months, waiting for the opportunity. The papers quoted Alice as saying, "I would rather she were dead than separated from me living." This was a strange, diabolical case, no doubt.

"Well, did you and Freda propose to have children?"

"No, we were not going to have children." For a moment, the doctor wondered if perhaps the friendship between the girls had ever taken on a more . . . *physical* aspect. Young girls hug and kiss all the time, but perhaps they had gone . . . further? He pushed the lurid thought from his head. That was the stuff of French novels; it was unthinkable for young ladies like Alice and Freda to actually engage in sex with each other.

New York Times article "A Most Shocking Crime," about the Mitchell-Ward murder. January 26, 1892. Factual discrepancies appear in several of the accounts.

"How do you know you were not?"

She leveled her gaze at him. "Oh, I know we were not."

THE WHOLE IDEA THAT TWO YOUNG WOMEN, raised in wealthy surroundings, could fall in love with each other was mystifying. The Mitchell-Ward murder trial rocked Memphis society in the first months of 1892, and daily news coverage of the event spread from coast to coast. The case sparked a flurry of articles on "sexual perversion" in medical journals, and the murder tale was soon retold in novels and at least one folk song.

All the doctors who examined Alice Mitchell concluded that she was "presently insane." After only twenty minutes of deliberation, the jury agreed—she was sent to an asylum in Bolivar, Tennessee. One Memphis paper wrote that "Discussion of the Mitchell-Ward murder has brought to light a number of similar cases of abnormal affection existing between persons of the same sex, differing only in that they did not end in the death of one 'lover' at the hands of the other."

But how should those strange relationships be understood? Or perhaps more to the point, how to describe those people? The word "homosexuality" was only beginning to be used that year in America by obscure medical journals—the term was mentioned neither in court nor in any of the press coverage of the Mitchell-Ward case from the 1890s. The word "lesbian" was uttered only rarely—the word's meaning would become commonly understood only in the 1930s or later.

Nevertheless, the American public was slowly beginning to acknowledge the existence of people among them who, inexplicably, were attracted to members of the same sex.

Way Back When

IT MAY BE HARD TO APPRECIATE that just over a hundred years ago, people didn't use the words "gay" and "lesbian" to describe a kind of sexuality. Of course, guys have been attracted to guys and gals have been attracted to gals since at *least* ancient times (the ancient Greeks left us explicit sex scenes on their pottery as proof, to take but one example). But the concept of "homosexuality" as a sexual orientation appeared in America during the late 1800s. We know that earlier, colonial Americans had homosex, but they didn't think about sexual identity the way we do today. Instead, "sodomy" was the term colonists used to describe various sexual acts that didn't lead to "procreation," or pregnancy. (In fact, sometimes the word "sodomy" was used for certain sexual acts, such as oral sex, that a man and a woman were physically able to do together.) The colonists' Puritan religion maintained that these acts were an offense against God. While religion was certainly a dominant

> CHAPTER 11
>
> *And be it further Enacted by the Authority aforesaid that if any Person shall be Legally Convicted of the Unnaturall Sin of Sodomy or Joyning with beasts, such persons shall be whipt and forfeit one third part of his or her Estate and worke Six months in the house of Correction at hard Labour and for the Second offence Imprisonment as aforesaid during Life.*

Chapter 11 from the statutes, or laws, of Pennsylvania during the seventeenth century.

reason for outlawing sodomy, historians have argued that colonists had a practical reason for doing so as well: it was particularly crucial for them to have children because their lives depended on it. Conditions in the North American wilderness were harsh, and the more workers they added to the community, the better their chances of survival.

In the early colonies, sodomy was no joke: it was a crime sometimes punishable by death. (Then again, so was witchcraft.) The colonists didn't believe that only certain people could be attracted to people of the same sex—they thought sodomy was an evil act by which *everyone* could be tempted.

That's the Spirit!

OF COURSE, COLONISTS WEREN'T THE ONLY ONES in America who were having same-sex relations at the time—American Indians were doing that, too. However, Indians have their own various religious and cultural beliefs, so their attitudes toward sex then were very different from those of the colonists. In fact, their ideas about gender were different, too. As ethnohistorian Walter Williams put it, in many Indian tribes, "biological sex is less important in gender classification than a person's desire—one's spirit."

While there are records of "special friendships" between American Indian men that were almost certainly sexual, the most striking image of homosexuality for white ethnographers came in the form of "berdaches." "Berdache" was a colonial term that described cross-dressing men found in as many as 130 different tribes. These men dressed as women, did recognized women's work like basket weaving and pottery, performed various sacred roles in the tribe, and often married non-berdache men, with whom they had sex (almost always passive anal sex). Berdaches were sometimes taunted, but they were generally respected—in many tribes, they were believed to have special spiritual abilities, including healing illnesses, predicting the weather, and providing spiritual protection. Williams noted that berdaches were thought to have "double vision, with the ability to see more clearly than a single gender prospective can provide." In some tribes, berdaches became matchmakers and marriage counselors. Usually berdaches were identified before puberty by the way they acted and the activities they preferred, and not later on by the question of whether they were sexually attracted to other men.

We'wha was a Zuni Indian berdache who made a big splash in 1886 when he traveled to Washington, D.C. There he met with various politicians (including President Grover Cleveland), all of whom assumed he was a female because of his clothing. But that was a rare exception to the rule, as colonizing whites had considered the berdache tradition to be the same thing as sodomy from the start. They persecuted berdaches mercilessly, and reports of such men declined significantly during the nineteenth and twentieth centuries. Nevertheless, the tradition has persisted to this day, and contemporary queer American Indians have adopted the term "Two Spirit" for themselves in lieu of the colonial word "berdache."

Historical records also indicate that there were female versions of berdaches, but unfortunately, there's little record of what kind of sexual relationships existed

Portrait of We'wha, a Zuni berdache, in native dress and holding a clay ceremonial prayer-meal basket. 1900.

between women in tribes. Historian Paula Gunn Allen argued that such women have traditionally been ignored by ethnographers with "a patriarchal worldview, in which lesbians are said not to exist and women are perceived as oppressed, burdened, powerless, and peripheral to interesting accounts of human affairs except in that they have babies." Nevertheless, she insisted that same-sex relationships between women must have existed in the American Indian past because they exist in the American Indian community today. She maintained that such relationships were possibly quite common, since tribal social arrangements separated men from women much of the time and the "primary personal unit tended to include members of one's own sex rather than members of the opposite sex."

Natural Laws

TWO HUNDRED YEARS AFTER THE EARLY COLONISTS, Americans during the nineteenth century were still being taught that procreation was the only natural and wholesome purpose of sex. However, while colonists had criminalized sodomy because they believed it was against God's will, later Americans kept it illegal because they thought it was a "crime against nature." American society—indeed, the world—had changed radically in those two centuries. During the eighteenth century, an intellectual movement known as the Enlightenment argued that reason was the main basis for authority, and it greatly influenced the nation's founders as they set up the country's laws. Then the Industrial Revolution brought a dizzying array of scientific discoveries and inventions, such as machine manufacturing, improved communication, and steam power for trains. These new developments transformed the way people lived. Rather than religion, science had become accepted as the objective source of knowledge about the world.

During the nineteenth century, doctors known as "sexologists" began studying and categorizing different kinds of sexual behavior. "Perversion" had been a term used by colonists to describe any sexual behavior that didn't follow the religious ideal of procreation, including sodomy. By the end of the nineteenth century, doctors were using the term "perversion" to mean behavior that strayed from what (they believed) most people did.

Male Bonding

THROUGHOUT THE 1800s, affection between men was expressed openly. Many photographs from the time show that men were not at all insecure about how they behaved toward each other in public—men often posed sitting on each other's laps, holding hands, or embracing. As one historian put it, "Boundaries between romantic friendship and erotic love were muddy." In fact, it wasn't a big deal for two men to share a bed, as a young Abraham Lincoln and storekeeper Joshua Speed did between 1837 and 1840.

Walt Whitman, one of America's greatest poets, was famous for advocating male-to-male companionship, or as he called it, "adhesiveness," or "the manly love of comrades." His masterwork of poetry, *Leaves of Grass*, waxed lyrical about such close relationships, as in this excerpt from the *Calamus* section:

> *For the one I love most lay sleeping by me*
> *under the same cover in the cool night,*
> *In the stillness in the autumn moonbeams*
> *his face was inclined toward me,*
> *And his arm lay lightly around my breast—*
> *and that night I was happy.*

Whitman himself had a series of intimate male companions throughout his life. Lewy Brown was a twenty-year-old Maryland farm boy wounded during the Civil War whom Whitman cared for at the Armory Square Hospital in Washington, D.C. Whitman once wrote to a friend, "Lew is so good, so affectionate—when I came away, he reached up his face, I put my arm around him, and we gave each other a long kiss, half a minute long." Perhaps Whitman's dearest "comrade" was Peter Doyle, to whom he sent bouquets of flowers and notes. Doyle would later say about Whitman, "His disposition was different. Woman in that sense never came into his head."

ABOVE: Two unidentified men. Circa 1860. OPPOSITE: Subjects unknown. Circa 1845–1850. A large number of photographs from the nineteenth century demonstrating affection between men have survived. However, the exact nature of their relationships remains unknown.

Best Friends Forever

WHEN FREDA WARD WAS MURDERED IN 1892, it was near the end of the Victorian age. This time period is named after Queen Victoria of England, and it is generally viewed as a time of moral prudery, with a lot of sexual repression. Any mention of sexual activity was considered inappropriate, sometimes even in conversations between a husband and wife, and men and women were largely separated from each other in their everyday activities. (Although one historian has famously pointed out that because Victorians went to such great lengths *not* to discuss or even acknowledge sex, this shows they were actually quite obsessed with it.)

Victorian society promoted intense same-sex friendships to keep men and women apart, lest they have sex (!). This allowed women and men to be very open about their feelings toward their same-sex friends. These "romantic friendships" were viewed quite positively; that's why Alice Mitchell and Freda Ward's amorous behavior toward each other seemed unremarkable—until the engagement rings and elopement plans, that is. In women's colleges, there was a tradition of "smashes" (sometimes also called "crushes" or "spoons") in which students courted each other. As a Yale College newspaper reported in 1873:

When a Vassar girl takes a shine to another, she straightaway enters upon a regular course of bouquet sendings, interspersed with tinted notes, mysterious packages of "Ridley's Mixed Candies," locks of hair perhaps, and many other tender tokens, until at last the object of her attentions is captured, the two women become inseparable, and the aggressor is considered by her circle of acquaintances as—smashed.

After college, a large number of these women moved in together and continued these pairings, sometimes called "Boston marriages." Many did so because it was harder for a working woman to earn the same amount of money as a man, and people at the time thought it was pretty sketchy for a woman to live alone. As more and more women received college degrees, the "New Woman" movement was born: a class of independent, educated women who typically worked in social reform or education. For women who graduated college in the early 1890s, only about half ever married, while 90 percent of non-college-educated women married. (Though the college graduates, too, would marry at a 90 percent rate by the end of the 1950s.) Many of these so-called spinsters lived as same-sex couples.

Jane Addams, a household name in turn-of-the-century America for her influential social work, had two major "romantic friendships" in her life. Ellen Gates Starr was her first; she was the woman with whom Addams started Chicago's famous Hull House in 1889, though they had become close twelve years before as students. The pair sent increasingly passionate letters to each other, and they celebrated the anniversary of their meeting for years (even after they later grew apart). In 1888, the two traveled to Europe together and visited Toynbee Hall in London, the settlement house that inspired Hull House.

The settlement house movement was a social justice movement that placed educated middle- and upper-class women and men in poor urban neighborhoods to learn about the local community's needs and help provide services. The staff members at Hull House all lived there, and Addams and Starr shared a bed in their own room. The house quickly developed to become a day-care center, a soup kitchen for the ill, a studio art space, a gymnasium, a library, a meeting hall, a kindergarten, and a vocational school for area residents. From the settlement house, Addams and the staff lobbied for legislative changes, supported social science research, campaigned against proposed racial segregation in Chicago schools, and pushed for what would become the first juvenile court in the country. Best of all, Hull House became an example for others: by 1900, almost one hundred settlement houses had been started in cities across the country. Addams would also go on to be president of the Women's International League for Peace and Freedom, advocating early on for a United Nations–style organization to bring peace and stability to the world. Her lifetime commitment to social justice earned her the 1931 Nobel Peace Prize.

Jane Addams with Mary Rozet Smith. Circa 1923–1930.

Though their professional partnership would continue for many years, the romance in Addams and Starr's friendship disappeared during the 1890s. It was then that Mary Rozet Smith, the daughter of a wealthy Chicago industrialist, became involved in the work of Hull House. Smith and Addams took an immediate "shine" to each other, and soon they were engaged in a romantic friendship of their own, one that would last forty years until Smith's death in 1934. (Addams would die fourteen months later.)

Did They or Didn't They?

IT'S A TRICKY TASK FOR HISTORIANS TODAY to figure out whether these close nineteenth-century romantic friendships ever became sexual relationships. Many surviving letters can seem sexually suggestive to us today, but people at the time often wrote letters in an exaggerated, passionate style. Even still, it's remarkable how hot-and-heavy the correspondences could be at times. In one unique case, two young South Carolinian men wrote letters to each other in 1826 that have raised a lot of questions for historians about early-nineteenth-century views on same-sex sexual relations. Thomas J. Withers wrote to James H. Hammond:

> *I feel some inclination to learn whether you yet sleep in your Shirt-tail, and whether you yet have the extravagant delight of poking and punching a writing Bedfellow with your long fleshen pole—the exquisite touches of which I have often had the honor of feeling? . . . Sir, you roughen the downy Slumbers of your Bedfellow. . . .*

A portrait of Rose Elizabeth Cleveland, sister of President Grover Cleveland. 1883.

Similarly, historians have uncovered sexually charged letters written later in the century by women in romantic friendships. The poet Emily Dickinson wrote to her friend Sue Gilbert in 1852:

> *Susie, will you indeed come home next Saturday, and be my own again, and kiss me as you used to? . . . I hope for you so much, and feel so eager for you, feel that I cannot* wait, *feel that* now *I must have you—that the expectation once more to see your face again, makes me feel hot and feverish, and my heart beats so fast.*

Likewise, in the correspondence between Rose Elizabeth Cleveland (sister of President Grover Cleveland) and wealthy widow Evangeline Marrs Simpson Whipple beginning in 1890, Cleveland recalled the times when

my Eve looks into my eyes with brief bright glances, with long rapturous embraces,—when her sweet life beneath and her warm enfolding arms appease my hunger, and quiet my [illegible] *and carry my body to the summit of joy, the end of search, the goal of love!*

Jane Addams once wrote to Mary Rozet Smith while on a lecture trip in Wisconsin, "Dearest, It made me quite homesick to go by the hotel [in Milwaukee] this morning. We did have a good time in it, didn't we?" Consider that whenever the pair of them traveled, Addams would wire ahead to be sure they would get a hotel room with a double bed. (But that fact alone gives us an interesting insight into the way Victorians thought—or didn't think—about sex: while the two clearly *preferred* to sleep in the same bed, their request didn't seem to raise eyebrows.) Whether or not they were sexually involved, Addams and Smith thought of themselves as a married couple. Another time Addams wrote, "You must know, dear, how I long for you all the time. . . . There is reason in the habit of married folk keeping together." After Smith's parents died, the two moved in together, and they even bought a Maine vacation house in both of their names (though almost all of it was paid for with Smith's money).

In Walt Whitman's case, there is some contradictory evidence. On one hand, Whitman kept notebooks in which he listed the names, ages, and descriptions of young men whom he had met (sometimes in the street) and often had "slept with" during the fall of 1862 in Brooklyn and 1863 in Washington. Even if the phrase "slept with" did not mean anything sexual at the time, it seems to be a pretty odd habit to pick up men on the street for some shared nap time. Also, in notebook entries from 1870, Whitman wrote, "Depress the adhesive nature. It is in excess—making life a torment . . . diseased and feverish disproportionate adhesiveness." Another time, he wrote about Peter Doyle, but replaced Doyle's name with a simple numerological code ("16.4") and later changed "him" to "her":

To give up absolutely & for good, from this present hour, this feverish, fluctuating, useless undignified pursuit of 16.4—too long (much too long) persevered in—so humiliating—It must come at last & had better come now—(It cannot possibly be a success).

Let there from this hour be no faltering, no getting [word erased] *at all henceforth, (not once, under any circumstances)—avoid seeing her, or meeting her, or any talk or explanations—or any meeting, whatever, from this hour forth, for life.*

On the other hand, late in Whitman's life an English writer repeatedly asked him in letters whether the homoerotic *Leaves of Grass* had a greater sexual meaning than generally recognized. Whitman eventually responded to deny any such "morbid inferences—wh' are disavow'd by me & seem damnable." However, Whitman went on to write, "The one great difference between you and me, temperament & theory, is *restraint*. . . ." Which, again, would suggest that Whitman experienced homosexual attraction, but by this time was more tight-lipped about his desires.

There were no alternative words in nineteenth-century American culture for what we today call "homosexuality"; it is unlikely that any of the people in romantic friendships would understand terms like "lesbian," "gay," or "homosexual." But some historians today consider women's romantic friendships as lesbian relationships anyway. Historian Lillian Faderman has argued that the modern term "lesbian" "accurately describes their committed domestic, sexual, and/or affectional experiences." In other words, "lesbian" as an adjective could include any woman who chooses another woman as the emotional center of her life, whether as domestic spouse, partner, or lifelong love. Similarly, historian Jonathan Ned Katz has pointed out that we limit ourselves too much by thinking about homosexuals and homosexuality only in terms of whether or not sex happens. That kind of reasoning would mean that someone is not a homosexual unless that person actually has sex. Does that also apply to a heterosexual? The words and categories we use today are inadequate to truly capture relationships in the past—and for that matter, the present.

LEFT: Poet Walt Whitman seated opposite Peter Doyle. Circa 1870s–1880s.

OPPOSITE: The English physician and writer Henry Havelock Ellis. Circa 1910.

What's Up, Doc?

MOST OF OUR TROUBLESOME CATEGORIES AND TERMS can be traced back to the Victorian sexologists who tried to classify sexual behavior. Although the word "homosexual" was first used in 1869 by a German doctor named Károly Mária Kertbeny in an open letter protesting Prussian sodomy laws, the term's first American appearance can be found in medical journals. One of the earliest such cases was an article by Chicago's Dr. James G. Kiernan, a man described by one historian as "the most prolific and influential U.S. sexologist." In an 1892 article (the same year as the Mitchell-Ward murder and trial), he defined "pure homosexuals" by stating their "general mental state is that of the opposite sex." At the same time, "heterosexuals" were defined as having "inclinations to both sexes" (today's "bisexual" inclinations) and "to abnormal methods of gratification." But homosexuality didn't immediately catch on as a term: "inversion" was most commonly used by early sexologists. Inversion better described what doctors generally believed was a condition in which stereotypical gender characteristics were reversed (boys acting like girls, and vice versa). Other early sexological terms included "Uranism" and "contrary sexual feeling," along with theories about homosexuals comprising a "third sex" or "intermediate sex."

Henry Havelock Ellis was a British sexologist whose book *Sexual Inversion*, published in 1897, was so controversial that it was banned in England. *Sexual Inversion* argued for greater acceptance of homosexuality, and that male "inverts" did not necessarily act stereotypically feminine. Ellis got that right, but then he drew stereotypically masculine conclusions about female "inverts," suggesting that they have "a decided taste and tolerance for cigars" and a "dislike and sometimes incapacity for needlework and other domestic occupations, while there is often some capacity for athletics." (Keep in mind that he also claimed that inverts' favorite color is green.) Though he thought homosexuals were born as such, Ellis blamed the "modern movement of emancipation" (the movement for getting women the right to vote, also called the women's suffrage movement) for an increase in female homosexuality, or at least a "spurious imitation" of sexual inversion. Many sexologists would continue to target suffrage activists as being "sexual perverts" because

Sigmund Freud. Circa 1900.

they threatened the established gender roles—a charge against feminists that would surface again and again throughout the next century. (Interestingly, Ellis was married to a female "invert," Edith Lees, whom he used as one of his anonymous case studies in the book.)

The influential ideas of an Austrian neurologist named Sigmund Freud, developed at the turn of the twentieth century, eventually eclipsed the theories of early sexologists. Freud's theory of psychoanalysis greatly influenced the fields of psychiatry and psychology and had an immeasurably huge effect on popular culture. In his psychoanalytic theory, Freud distinguished between "sexual aim" (how a person prefers to have sex, whether it be oral sex, a passive role, etc.) and "sexual object" (whom to have sex with, whether male or female). He argued that all people were bisexual on some level, and that homosexual tendencies were normal in every person's sexual development, the goal of which was supposed to be heterosexuality. He didn't draw any definitive conclusions for *why* some people experienced a "certain arrest of sexual development" in the homosexual phase, but many of his followers would argue that homosexuals could be "treated" by undoing whatever supposed childhood traumas led to this condition. Freud himself doubted that homosexuals could be turned heterosexual, and he wrote to an American mother in 1935 that he believed homosexuality was "nothing to be ashamed of, no vice, no degradation, it cannot be classified as an illness."

On one hand, early sexologists were helpful in trying to change views about "sodomy" because they considered "sexual inversion" to be a medical condition, not a sin or a crime. On the other hand, most psychiatrists told homosexual patients that they were sick. This soon led to inhumane "treatments" (read: "torture") such as castrations, lobotomies, and electroshock "therapy." (In 1935, one New York University researcher would report to the American Psychological Association to have had some limited success in treating one patient's "homosexual neurosis" by administering electric shocks of "intensities considerably higher than those usually employed on human subjects.") Moreover, the stigma of disease would remain with gay people for many decades. Homosexuals during that time often did not believe they *could* question a medical diagnosis; they could not imagine that they were actually "normal" and that their feelings were "natural."

The detailed discussions between early sexologists about these "pathological conditions" were fairly hidden, however, from the general public. Some doctors would switch to Latin when describing the various sexual activities of homosexuals in professional journals, so that nonprofessionals would be less likely to read about them. Nevertheless, these terms and categories leaked into popular culture, becoming commonplace by the close of World War I, when "romantic friendships" had become rare for their increasing association with homosexuality.

Making a Pass

WHEN ALICE MITCHELL TOLD DR. TURNER that she could dress as a man and find work to support herself and Freda Ward, she wasn't (necessarily) off her rocker. The Victorian age saw an interesting result from the many restrictions on women: women who disguised themselves and lived as men, a phenomenon known as "passing." These women chose to pursue their lives as men for a wide variety of reasons, including broader economic opportunities, self-identification as a man, the desire for political rights—or, of course, the ability to pursue other women. In many places, dressing as a man was a criminal offense, and women took great risks in choosing to pass. Usually working class, these women often took physical jobs and had to teach themselves how to act like men—which involved learning how to saunter, how to spit, how to chew tobacco and smoke cigars, and, of course, how to flirt with women.

Babe Bean. Drawing from the Stockton *Evening Mail.* October 9, 1897.

Murray Hall, an influential politician in New York City's Democratic Party during the 1880s and 1890s, passed as a man for twenty-five years. She married twice, and even raised an adopted daughter. Reportedly, both marriages had been troubled ones because Hall was "too attentive to women." In the end, Hall was desperate to keep her secret safe—when she discovered she had breast cancer, she tried to treat it herself and only agreed to see a doctor days before she died.

When a man calling himself "Babe Bean" was discovered to be physically female in Stockton, California, in 1897, she became a media sensation. Stockton's Bachelor's Club even made her an honorary member, and she was hired by the local paper as a celebrity reporter. When the Spanish-American War broke out the next year, Bean left Stockton to serve as a lieutenant under the name "Jack Garland," and then afterward moved to San Francisco where she spent the rest of her life aiding the homeless and the hungry. Not until she died at the age of sixty-six in 1936 was Garland revealed to be the same person as Babe Bean. Also, it was finally learned that she was born Elvira Virginia Mugarrieta, the daughter of the founder of San Francisco's Mexican consulate and reportedly the granddaughter of a Louisiana Supreme Court justice.

Wilde Thing

Oscar Wilde and Lord Alfred Douglas. Circa 1894.

UNFORTUNATELY, IT SEEMS that most public discussion of homosexuality during the Victorian era centered on scandals. Cases like the murder of Freda Ward helped create a stereotype that linked same-sex attraction to violence and inevitable tragedy. The best-known such scandal was the trial of Oscar Wilde.

Wilde was a playwright living in London, England, who was world famous for his colorful personality and witty plays, including *The Importance of Being Earnest* and *An Ideal Husband.* Wilde was enamored with a younger man named Lord Alfred Douglas. The two had an intimate (though troubled) relationship for several years. Though Wilde was married and a father, he and Douglas would arrange to have sex with lower-class young men in exchange for gifts or money. Meanwhile, Douglas's father, the marquess of Queensberry, was enraged that his son was spending so much time with the controversial and flamboyant Wilde. The marquess began intimidating and harassing the playwright. Wilde responded with a libel suit, which he lost, thereby leaving himself open to charges of "gross indecency." Though given plenty of opportunities to escape England, Wilde stayed, and during his trial in 1895, he stated an eloquent defense of love between men. Nevertheless, he was convicted and sentenced to two years of hard labor. Wilde served his prison time and died a few years later, in 1900, a penniless and broken man. His trial was well covered in American newspapers, although some newspapers, like *The New York Times*, considered his crime too heinous to describe. In the newspaper's extensive coverage of Wilde's case, from the trial until his death, neither the crime nor the charge was ever named. (The *Times* would not print the word "homosexuality" until as late as 1926.)

Slumming

Loop-the-Loop, a fairy prostitute from Brooklyn. 1906.

DESPITE THE CODED, EVASIVE LANGUAGE of newspapers and polite society during the Victorian age, the general public was not entirely clueless about sexual relations between members of the same sex. Historians such as George Chauncey and Jonathan Ned Katz have uncovered evidence of a thriving homosexual culture in Victorian era New York that was quite visible to the rest of the city. The saloons in the area known today as the Lower East Side of Manhattan, particularly along the Bowery, were disreputable establishments where "fairies" could be found. "Fairy" was a derogatory term even then (as was almost any term for a homosexual), but one that was accepted by "fairies" as a name for themselves. In this era of the "sexual invert," it was commonly believed that any man performing so-called passive roles in a sex act would be a lot like a woman: wearing makeup or women's clothing, having an effeminate manner, and being attracted to "masculine" men. That was the image presented to the public by the fairies of the Bowery, who were often prostitutes. It became quite popular for "respectable" people (both hetero- and homosexual) to go "slumming" along the Bowery, which was their term for touring the titillating saloons and hotels found there.

2 : GOOD TIMES . . . & BAD TIMES
1910–1939

"You're neither unnatural, nor abominable, nor mad; you're as much a part of what people call nature as anyone else."

—STEPHEN GORDON IN *THE WELL OF LONELINESS* BY RADCLYFFE HALL, 1928

Chicago, 1925

AFTER A GOOD NIGHT DOWNTOWN, Henry was just glad to finally get some sleep. It was already two in the morning, and he would have to be up in good time for work at the post office. Oh, wait—today was Sunday, wasn't it? He could sleep in.

There was a knock on the door. Henry cursed under his breath. What on earth could his nosy landlady want at this hour?

When he opened the door, Henry saw it wasn't his landlady. Two men stood before him, wearing long coats and decidedly unfriendly expressions. The first held a large box. "Henry Gerber?" he asked.

"Yes . . ." Henry answered, uncertainly.

The man identified himself as a city detective, and he waved toward the other man, saying he was a reporter from the *Examiner*. The detective brusquely pushed past Henry, asking, "Where's the boy?"

Henry was flabbergasted. "What boy?" The detective just scowled and began moving about the apartment. He lifted up Henry's typewriter from the desk, and dropped it into his box.

"What's going on here? What are you doing with my typewriter?" asked Henry.

"I have orders from my precinct captain. I'm taking you back to the station."

"But I haven't done anything!" cried Henry, feeling the panic rise in his throat.

The detective ignored him, pulling Henry's notary public diploma from the wall and adding it to the box. The reporter stood inside the door, scribbling in his pad.

"I . . . I don't understand. What are you looking for—don't take those, I need those!" The detective stuffed Henry's bookkeeping records into the box.

"Do you have a warrant? Aren't you supposed to have a warrant?" Henry asked, his voice breaking.

Then the detective walked over to the cabinet in the corner, and Henry felt the blood drain from his face.

"No, no, no—you can't go there—" But it was too late.

"Bingo," the detective said, peering inside. He pulled out the stack of papers and shook his head, disgusted. The reporter hurried over to look. They paged through copies of the first two issues of *Friendship and Freedom*, the newsletter for the Chicago Society for Human Rights, the group Henry started last year.

It would all be over now, Henry knew. This was the end.

At the station, the detective shoved Henry into a cell without a word. Henry lay awake, thinking about how such injustice was possible in the United States of America in this day and age. He had spent three years in Germany serving with the U.S. Army of Occupation following World War I. There, in Coblenz on the Rhine, Henry had subscribed to German homophile magazines, with contributors who wrote openly about minority rights for homosexuals. And those trips to Berlin—what an incredible city! What a progressive, sexually liberated city! And what fun he had had there.

Henry knew, he just *knew*, he had found his calling. He would deliver freedom to the oppressed homosexual, as Abraham Lincoln had done for the slaves. So upon returning home from Europe, he formed the Society for Human Rights, which would educate the public about homosexuality and work to change discriminatory laws. Henry tried to gather members for the organization's work—but it was harder than he had expected. Some of his friends were too scared. Others just didn't care. Others claimed to like the fact that their sexual activities were illegal—it made it more exciting, they said.

The handful of people he did manage to interest were all very poor: John preached brotherly love to small groups of blacks. Al was an indigent "laundry queen," and Ralph had a job with the railroad. They were the national officers. Realizing that he was the only literate member, Henry arranged for the organization's charter from the state of Illinois. He paid for and wrote *Friendship and Freedom*. Henry didn't mind, though—he would be remembered and honored for it someday. . . .

In the morning, the police allowed Henry to make a phone call. He called his boss, who was unusually quiet throughout the conversation. Henry had once translated a work of philosophy from German for him, but he wasn't sure how far that favor would get him today. In the end, Henry was told that his status would be fixed as "absent on leave."

Then, one of the friendlier policemen showed Henry a copy of the day's *Examiner*. Splashed across the front page was the headline, "Strange Sex Cult Exposed." The article claimed that Henry and John the preacher had been arrested at the home of the society's vice president, Al. According to the article, Al's wife had called the police because Al and his friends had performed "strange sex acts" in front of her and the children. The fact that Al even had a wife and children was news to Henry. The article also mentioned that in the apartment a sex cult's pamphlet was found, which "urged men to leave their wives and children."

Even in the midst of his despair, Henry felt his blood boil.

EVENTUALLY, HENRY WAS RELEASED on $1,000 bail, and his lawyer managed to get the charges dropped due to the warrantless search and a complete lack of evidence. Nevertheless, the scandalous news story destroyed the Society for Human Rights, and Henry was fired from his job at the post office for "conduct unbecoming a postal worker." He would continue to write passionately in defense of homosexuality in various publications for decades, both under his own name and the pen name "Parisex."

Henry Gerber was the first American to attempt to organize homosexuals in a political way. But he was a pioneer well ahead of his time—other than an unsuccessful plan by a German immigrant in New York to start up an organization for "inverts" in 1930, there would be no similar attempt for the next twenty-five years. The first half of the twentieth century was a very difficult time for most homosexual Americans—a time when few could live openly as themselves. Across America, thousands lived quiet lives and left very little record of their sexuality. (Although in one rare exception, a group of twenty-five middle-class women in Salt Lake City, Utah, left written interviews and an analysis of their covert lesbian community during the 1920s and 1930s to a historian.)

However, there was one place where homosexuals were able to at least gather in public and gain visibility: New York City, then the undisputed center of homosexual life in America.

We're Here, We're "Queer"

AS AMERICA ENTERED the new century, most people still thought all homosexual men were by definition highly feminine, like the "fairies" who could be found in New York's less-reputable neighborhoods. But by the 1910s and 1920s, middle-class men had developed the beginnings of what historian George Chauncey calls the "gay world" in New York.

Homosexual men of the middle class didn't see themselves as being at all like the crude prostitutes who hung out in saloons and dockyards. Sure, these men recognized their own similarities to fairies in their attraction for men, but they didn't wear women's clothing and they had respectable jobs. These men tried to set themselves apart by calling themselves "queer." "Queer wasn't derogatory. . . . it just meant you were different," recalled one homosexual man about New York in the 1920s. The lines weren't clearly drawn between the two groups, but queer middle-class men were able to blend into the social life of the city better than "fairies." One method was what Chauncey described as a "pronounced Anglophilia," a social style that imitated English nobles—it was urbane, witty, and refined. This sort of persona helped a man mask his homosexuality. Whenever he was ridiculed for being effeminate, he could "dismiss such ridicule as a sign of lower-class brutishness." At this time, the police were more concerned about shutting down fairy hangouts, so queer men were largely free to build their own culture, invisible to an ignorant public. In the city's rooming houses, cafeterias, baths, and speakeasies later on, these men gradually created a strong social network that would serve as the basis for New York's "gay world."

A cartoon depicting Greenwich Village as a center of lesbian and gay life. From *Broadway Brevities*. June 6, 1932.

Bohemians at the Gate

IN THE 1910s, Greenwich Village in New York City became famous as *the* neighborhood for artists, poets, socialists, and "free love" radicals. These bohemians prided themselves on their tolerance for anything unorthodox, and homosexuality certainly fit the bill. Historian Lillian Faderman noted, "It was, in fact, bohemian chic for a woman to be able to admit to a touch of lesbianism." But even in this anything-goes atmosphere, most Villagers thought Freud was right; homosexuality should be a phase—anything more than a little experimentation was a problem. Poet Edna St. Vincent Millay was an early lesbian figure in Village artistic circles. At a party, Millay complained of a headache, and a psychoanalyst asked her whether perhaps it might have been caused by a repressed "occasional impulse toward a person of [her] own sex?" She replied, "Oh, you mean I'm homosexual! Of course I am, and heterosexual too, but what's that got to do with my headache?" Millay and other lesbians felt the pressure toward heterosexuality; she took some male lovers (one of whom recommended psychoanalysis as a cure for her lesbian interests), and she eventually married. However, she said later that she and her husband "lived like two bachelors," and she continued to have affairs with women.

Anarchist Emma Goldman was another fixture of the Greenwich Village scene, one who spoke out in defense of homosexuality as early as 1915 in her lecture tours around the country. Anarchism was a political movement that hoped to transform society by removing the influence of authority. Goldman wrote in her autobiography that although other anarchists got upset that she brought up homosexuality, "To me anarchism was not a mere theory for a distant future. It was a living influence to free us from inhibitions, internal no less than external, and from the destructive barriers that separate man from man." Although Goldman received sexually explicit letters from fellow anarchist Almeda Sperry, she did not consider herself a lesbian and seems to have been otherwise heterosexual in her many love affairs.

ABOVE: Edna St. Vincent Millay, the winner of the Pulitzer Prize for Best Volume of Verse in 1922. February 16, 1925.

LEFT: Emma Goldman, standing on a car, speaks about birth control in Union Square, New York City. May 21, 1916.

In the mid-1910s, elaborate costume balls were held annually in Webster Hall by the bohemians of Greenwich Village to raise money for the Liberal Club. Undercover investigators noted over the years that an increasingly "prominent feature of these dances [was] the number of male perverts who attend them." Indeed, by the 1920s, homosexual men were throwing their own balls at Webster Hall, the Savoy, and Madison Square Garden. The black neighborhood of Harlem also hosted spectacular drag balls in the 1920s that attracted thousands of participants and spectators.

Some heterosexual Greenwich Village residents resented that the famous neighborhood was becoming associated with homosexuals. One Villager wrote in 1922 that the Liberal Club balls were being hurt "by the admission of stags and certain mincing undesirables from uptown who love to exhibit themselves in dainty effulgence." Editor Malcolm Cowley lived in the Village in the 1920s, and he imagined a writer's revolution in which "you would set about hanging policemen from the lamp posts . . . and beside each policeman would be hanged a Methodist preacher, and beside each preacher a pansy poet." In 1936, a venomous article in *Current Psychology and Psychoanalysis* noted the influence of homosexuals on the character of the neighborhood: "Greenwich Village, which was once a happy, carefree abode of struggling young writers and artists, inhabited by many of America's literati, is now a roped-off section of what showmen would call 'Freak Exhibits.'"

The Great War

THOUGH HISTORIANS HAVE NOT YET UNCOVERED the extent of it, World War I had a freeing effect on Americans' sexuality. As more and more men entered the army, the sudden decrease in the number of available bachelors took some pressure off young women to marry. Also more and more people accepted the idea—first proposed by Freud—that repressing sexual desire was unhealthy. It has been suggested that women during the war felt freer to explore sexuality with each other than before. At the same time, the military plucked young men out of their homes and families and put them into a single-sex environment that didn't have the same kind of supervision—which actually increased the chances that they would meet homosexuals and be able to act on same-sex desires. New York City was the major departure point for sailors on their way to Europe, and many young men from all over the country suddenly found themselves in a city that included visibly identifiable homosexuals, such as the fairies along the waterfront and in Times Square, as well as the "artistic" homosexuals in Greenwich Village. Additionally, while in Europe, these soldiers saw homosexual life in Paris and Berlin on a much more developed scale than in America—indeed, Germany by this time had a full-fledged gay rights movement (which had inspired Henry Gerber

A draft parade for World War I heads up Fifth Avenue near Forty-first Street in New York City. The lions of the New York Public Library are on the far left, and the spire of St. Patrick's can be seen farther up the avenue. 1917.

after the war). Upon returning to the United States, it is believed that many homosexual men chose to settle in New York.

The high numbers of young men hanging around the streets of New York at this time became a source of concern for antivice societies. These private organizations had been formed around the turn of the century in response to urban problems such as prostitution, problems believed to have been caused by the city's rapid growth and increased immigration. The Committee of Fourteen and the Society for the Prevention of Crime were two antivice societies that investigated the Bowery saloons and hotels and pressured the police to close them down. The Society for the Suppression of Vice focused on uncovering the underground homosexual culture of the city during World War I, organizing police raids on bathhouses and other locations where homosexuals gathered. The carefully documented records of the societies' undercover investigators are among the most revealing sources historians today use to understand the hidden gay culture in New York during the first few decades of the twentieth century.

During World War I, the navy investigated the presence of homosexuals at the Newport, Rhode Island, navy training station, inadvertently revealing that the distinctions between being "queer" and "normal" were changing. In order to find and build a case against "queers" in the military, the navy had volunteer "decoys," sailors who were assumed to be heterosexual, go to the YMCA (where queers were rumored to hang out), and allow themselves to be seduced. "Trade" was a term used to describe heterosexually identified men who played the "masculine," or "active," role in sexual encounters that queers would initiate. (Thus, "queer" in this context meant something a bit different from how middle-class men in New York were using the term, where it didn't always imply a sexual role.) But as the cases of thirty-six arrested men went to trial, the assumptions and means of the investigation became increasingly controversial. During questioning, it became less clear who a queer was—did the fact that the decoys volunteered to commit homosexual acts make *them* homosexual? The idea that queers were only men who took the "passive" role in a sex act was slowly changing to a general belief that any man who was willing to engage in sex with another man was queer. Moreover, the extreme methods used to find these men drew criticism. The public was so scandalized that two other investigations were conducted, including one by the Senate Naval Affairs Committee that condemned the handling of the situation by naval officials—including the assistant secretary of the navy at the time, Franklin D. Roosevelt.

Prohibition Brings Freedom

IRONICALLY, THE RATIFICATION OF THE EIGHTEENTH AMENDMENT to the U.S. Constitution, the "Prohibition Amendment," brought down the influence of antivice societies. There had been many campaigns to curb Americans' heavy drinking habits ever since colonial times, but during the nineteenth century the temperance movement became particularly successful in manipulating the media, scientific instruction in schools, and the political process to convince many Americans that alcohol was the root of many of the country's problems. With America's entry into the First World War, temperance groups seized upon widespread antiforeign (particularly anti-German) feelings, pointing out that many of the country's breweries were founded by German-Americans. By 1919, temperance groups had succeeded in getting an amendment to the U.S. Constitution passed and ratified to outlaw the manufacture and sale of alcohol throughout the United States.

This Prohibition law was very unpopular in New York City, as it was elsewhere, and lawbreaking was widespread. Organized crime took over the alcohol trade, and corruption increased dramatically. This general disrespect for the law loosened the rigid social rules from the Victorian era, and the surveillance activities of antivice societies lost favor with the general public. Later on, the economic difficulties brought on by the Great Depression ended much of the private financial support given to antivice societies.

Speakeasies were hidden, illegal bars that tolerated all kinds of unconventional behavior, and some New York speakeasies specifically catered to homosexuals. One famous tearoom and speakeasy in Greenwich Village was run by a Polish immigrant named Eva Kotchover (also known as Eve Addams or Eve Adams). A sign was posted on the door: "Men are admitted but not welcome." The club, known as Eve's Hangout, was very popular, and Kotchover held poetry readings that were "jammed" with people. Unfortunately, the club's popularity also got the

A man kneeling on the pavement, next to a sign showing the way to a speakeasy, during Prohibition in America. 1925.

attention of the police—they raided the club in 1925, charged Kotchover with disorderly conduct, and found a collection of her short stories, titled *Lesbian Love*, which they deemed obscene. She served a year in the workhouse and was deported to her native Poland—though she reportedly moved to Paris soon after and opened a lesbian club there.

TOP: A group of women, many dressed as men in tuxedos, and some with monocles, sit, talk, laugh, and kiss at Le Monocle, a famous night club for women. Paris, 1920s.

BOTTOM: Alice B. Tolkas and Gertrude Stein in an open car. Undated photograph.

Gay Paree

PARIS WAS A DRAW FOR DISENCHANTED American citizens, too, during the 1920s. These expatriates formed a social web that sometimes took advantage of the highly developed gay subculture to be enjoyed there. Lesbian writer Natalie Clifford Barney once stated, "Paris has always seemed to me the only city where you can live and express yourself as you please." A wealthy heiress, Barney made her residence in Paris a famous artistic salon, or informal meeting place, for more than fifty years. Sometimes called the "Amazon," Barney was famously a big flirt, and she openly advocated having many lovers. At one point, she and one of her lovers traveled to the Greek island of Lesbos with visions of re-creating an ancient lesbian school of poetry—but the relationship ended soon after, effectively scrapping the plans.

Gertrude Stein was also a writer and self-proclaimed "genius" who held a salon in Paris (along with her lifelong companion Alice B. Toklas) that hosted such famous artists and writers as Pablo Picasso, Ernest Hemingway, Sherwood Anderson, and Henri Matisse. Novelist Djuna Barnes, who had satirized bohemian life in Greenwich Village in the 1910s, satirized her lesbian experiences in Paris in her 1928 book, *Ladies Almanack*. She later published the novel *Nightwood*, which was really about her tortured eight-year relationship in Paris with artist Thelma Wood.

Swingin' Harlem in the Jazz Age

YOU DIDN'T HAVE TO GO ALL THE WAY to Paris "to live and express yourself as you please" during the 1920s. New York City's neighborhood of Harlem became a popular entertainment district for both white and black people during that decade. Sometimes this entertainment was predicated on racist ideas, that somehow the African Americans of Harlem were "primitive" and more in touch with their wild side—the entertainment district on West 133rd Street was even nicknamed "Jungle Alley." Harlem offered white spectators the opportunity to witness something "exotic" (however inauthentic), and release themselves from the social restrictions of their own communities. Antivice organizations largely ignored this poor black neighborhood, so liquor and prostitution flourished. Sex inevitably became part of the attraction for whites who went "slumming"—particularly with "rent parties," or parties at private apartments that charged admission for a night of dancing, jazz, bootleg liquor, and sometimes sex acts.

Homosexuality was part of Harlem's relative sexual freedom. Elaborate drag balls, described by poet Langston Hughes as "spectacles of color," attracted thousands of spectators and participants from as far away as Philadelphia, Atlantic City, Pittsburgh, and Boston. Some nightclub shows featured openly homosexual performers, such as the Clam House's Gladys Bentley, who wore a tuxedo and top hat as she sang and played the piano. Bentley flaunted a lesbian persona onstage, and was rumored to have married another woman in a New Jersey ceremony (although decades later, she would publicly renounce her homosexuality).

Several Harlem speakeasies catered to a homosexual clientele, including a couple of bars that attracted cross-dressers. Artist Richard Bruce Nugent occasionally visited a speakeasy where he found "rough queers—the kind that fought better than truck drivers and swished better than Mae West." (Mae West was an actress who was famous at the time for delivering sexually suggestive lines.)

The nightspot that best evokes glittering images of Harlem in the 1920s and 1930s is the Cotton Club. Circa 1920s–1940s.

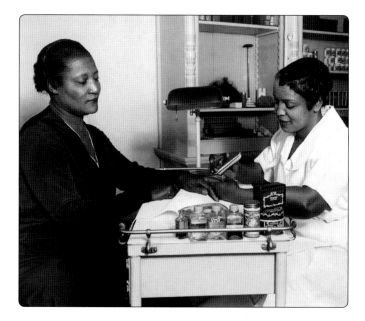

A'Lelia Walker, daughter of Madame C. J. Walker, gets a manicure at one of her mother's beauty shops. Circa 1920–1931.

The relative freedom of Harlem's nightlife drew many homosexual as well as heterosexual spectators, including celebrities such as lesbian heiress Louisa Dupont Carpenter Jenny, the colorful, bisexual actress Tallulah Bankhead, and novelist Carl Van Vechten, who supported many Harlem artists and popularized the neighborhood to many whites through his writing. A'Lelia Walker was a wealthy black lesbian who hosted spectacular parties in her Harlem home that were attended by European royalty and New York's high society, as well as Harlem's own writers and artists. She also hosted less reputable parties: Mabel Hampton, a dancer in the 1920s, later remembered those "funny parties—there were men and women, straight and gay. . . . Some people had clothes on, some didn't. People would hug and kiss on pillows and do anything they wanted to do. You could watch if you wanted to. Some came to watch, some came to play. You had to be cute and well-dressed to get in."

Among women singers in Harlem, bisexuality was an integral part of the scene. Gertrude "Ma" Rainey, Bessie Smith, Alberta Hunter, Josephine Baker, and Ethel Waters all carried on affairs with women. Rainey, a performer known as the "Mother of the Blues," was arrested in 1925 for hosting an "indecent party" in her apartment with women in her chorus, and she later used the publicity surrounding the arrest to promote her next album. Her song "Prove It On Me Blues" included the lyrics

> *Went out last night with a crowd of my friends,*
> *They must have been women, 'cause I don't like no men.*
> *Wear my clothes just like a fan, Talk to gals just like any old man*
> *'Cause they say I do it, ain't nobody caught me, Sure got to prove it on me.*

Lucille Bogan's song "BD Women's Blues" (performed under the name Bessie Jackson) was similarly open about lesbianism. "BD" stood for "bulldagger," a common term used to describe a butch lesbian. According to music historians, a song called "BD's Dream" was one of the most frequently played songs at rent parties.

Despite the apparent public appeal of these lesbian images, Harlem women were not free of social disapproval. Just as in the bohemian circles of Greenwich Village, many of these women married. Historian Lillian Faderman wrote:

> *These women, who did not take great pains to pretend to exclusive heterosexuality, must have believed that in their own sophisticated circles of Harlem, bisexuality was seen as interesting and provocative. Although unalloyed homosexuality may still have connoted in 1920s Harlem the abnormality of 'a man trapped in a woman's body,' bisexuality seems to have suggested that a woman was super-sexy.*

For Harlem men who were "in the life" (homosexual), being open about it was no easier than for the women. Many of the leading figures of the Harlem Renaissance, a flowering of African American art, music, and literature, were homosexual—including artist Richard Bruce Nugent, college professor Alain Locke, sculptor Richmond Barthé, writer Wallace Thurman, and poet Countee Cullen. Though no conclusive evidence has been uncovered, many in Harlem also assumed poet Langston Hughes to be homosexual. There were several private apartments around Harlem that were known for their wild homosexual parties, and Alexander Gumby ran a Harlem literary salon known as "Gumby's Bookstore"

TOP: Group portrait of blues singer Gertrude "Ma" Rainey and her Georgia Jazz Band. Chicago, Illinois, 1923.

BOTTOM: Poet Countee Cullen. 1925.

(because of the many books lining the walls) that was frequented by homosexual men. However, Harlem men were not immune to social pressure, and many chose marriage as a disguise. Though Cullen was in a lifelong relationship with a schoolteacher named Harold Jackman, he married twice, the first time to the daughter of black leader W. E. B. DuBois, a founder of the National Association for the Advancement of Colored People (NAACP). These men knew well what could happen to their careers if word got out: when DuBois's protégé Augustus Granville Dill was arrested for soliciting men for sex in a public restroom, Dill's career as the business editor of the NAACP's *The Crisis* was finished. Nevertheless, it was no secret among the Harlem elite that many of the Renaissance leaders were homosexual.

The Great White Way . . . to Jail

ABOVE: Mae West in a scene from *Sex*. February 1927.

OPPOSITE: Cast of the play *The Children's Hour*. Circa 1935.

EANWHILE, IN MIDTOWN New York, Broadway was at its most popular during the 1920s, with one season putting on two hundred and fifty different shows at seventy theaters. (In contrast, there were only fifty-four shows during the 2005–2006 season.) In the twenties, several plays opened that notoriously dealt with homosexuality. As early as 1923, Sholom Asch's Broadway play *God of Vengeance* had a lesbian theme that caused the producer, director, and cast to be arrested for obscenity. More famously, in 1926, Edouard Bourdet's play *The Captive*, a story of a married woman haunted by homosexual desire, opened on Broadway. The producer and cast were arrested four months later in 1927 after it generated sufficient controversy. Performances of *The Captive* were shut down in San Francisco, Los Angeles, and Detroit. At the same time, saucy writer/actress Mae West planned to open a play on Broadway about queer life called *The Drag*, for which it was said she recruited forty homosexual chorus boys at a Greenwich Village speakeasy. Unfortunately, the play was banned before West even got the chance. In 1927, the New York state legislature passed a bill outlawing plays "depicting or dealing with, the subject of sex degeneracy, or sex perversion," which at the time meant homosexuality.

Nevertheless, Lillian Hellman's debut play, *The Children's Hour*, opened in 1934. The play describes the terrible fate of two schoolteachers who are accused of lesbianism by a troublesome student. The Broadway production ran for more than seven hundred performances, but when the play was adapted as a movie in 1936, the story was rewritten as a heterosexual love triangle and renamed *These Three*. By this time, Hollywood production studios had adopted the Production

Code, a set of rules governing language and behavior on-screen designed to control the "morality" of motion pictures. "Sex perversion or any inference to it" was strictly banned, as were many other topics deemed unsuitable. The ban would remain in place for the next thirty years.

The Well of Notoriety

As notorious as these theatrical productions were, perhaps the best-known artistic work to describe the lesbian experience in the first half of the twentieth century was Radclyffe Hall's *The Well of Loneliness*, published in 1928. The novel describes the life of "Stephen" Gordon, a wealthy, masculine Englishwoman who falls in love with a woman named Mary Llewellyn. Though the book ends on a sad note (which was typical for books dealing with homosexuality for most of the twentieth century), it was an early sympathetic portrait of a lesbian written by a lesbian. Moreover, the book called for greater social acceptance of "inverts." The book was banned in Great Britain for its lesbian content, and a U.S. court deemed it obscene shortly thereafter. (The raciest line of the book reads, "and that night they were not divided.") However, a U.S. appellate court struck down the ruling in 1929, making headlines. The book's infamy made it successful and therefore

available to lesbians all over the country. As historian Lillian Faderman noted, "Each year saw the production of new novels that were even clearer than Radclyffe Hall's book had been in the treatment of lesbian sexuality. Obviously the public had a taste for such fare, which, unlike Hall's work . . . presented lesbians as vampires and carnivorous flowers."

Crazy for Pansies

IN THE 1920s, a Brooklyn-born teenager named Victor Eugene James "Gene" Malin performed as a female impersonator in Greenwich Village clubs and drag balls around the city. He used the name "Jean Malin" (or sometimes "Imogene Wilson"), and he developed a following of devoted fans. Malin got his big break at one of the city's fanciest clubs, Club Abbey, in spring of 1930. There he changed from being a female impersonator to being a "pansy" host; he was dressed in men's clothing, but acted the feminine, sharp-witted stereotype of a "pansy." Six feet tall and two hundred pounds, Malin had an imposing onstage presence—rumors circulated about how he single-handedly beat up a group of four hecklers at a cafeteria one night, only to complain afterward about the sorry state of his clothing. Though he was an object of fascination

ABOVE: Prizewinning writer Radclyffe Hall (standing), whose novel *The Well of Loneliness* was originally banned in Great Britain for its sympathetic approach to female homosexuality, with Lady Una Trowbridge. They lived together as lovers for many years. 1927.

BELOW: Jean Malin with female impersonator "Helen Morgan Jr." at Club Abbey in New York. A cartoon from *Vanity Fair*. February 1931.

for audience members, Malin did not let himself be an object of ridicule—in fact, part of his show was to use his wit to get back at men in the audience who yelled insults at him. His incredible popularity caused a wave of imitations across clubs all over the city, and the sudden vogue for "pansy" acts even led to the opening of a Broadway nightclub late in 1930 called the Pansy Club.

Meanwhile, America was in the midst of the Great Depression, a worldwide economic downturn that began with the stock market crash of 1929. International trade, personal incomes, tax revenue, and profits all fell, while unemployment and poverty became nationwide crises. Suddenly, the party atmosphere of the rollicking 1920s seemed excessive, if not offensive. As fast as the "pansy craze" had started, within a year it was pretty much over. Public opinion had shifted, and newspapers began a campaign criticizing the new stage acts. Several states would pass legislation outlawing "female impersonators" onstage, and New York officials extended the theater ban on "sexual degeneracy" to nightclubs and cabarets. Pansy emcees were quickly replaced by traditional acts. (Jean Malin moved to Hollywood and a few years later died tragically in a car accident.) In 1931, the national RKO chain of theaters even banned the use of the words "fairy" or "pansy" in performances. The New York City police also shut down the elaborate annual drag balls in the city (though the biggest of the balls, located in Harlem, would escape the police's attention a few months later—and in 1930s Chicago, semiannual drag balls were assigned police protection).

Prohibition II

THIS WAS JUST THE BEGINNING of a dark decade for homosexuals. When Prohibition was repealed with the 21st Amendment to the U.S. Constitution in 1933, a new mechanism was introduced by states for monitoring the "moral order" of the public: liquor licensing. Part of the argument for Prohibition had been the number of social problems associated with saloons, such as prostitution and disorderly public behavior. During the repeal, lawmakers were very careful in trying to prevent saloons from coming back. States mandated that businesses wanting to serve alcohol had to apply for a liquor license. That license could be revoked if certain conditions were not met, particularly the conduct of patrons at any establishment where liquor was being served. The mere *presence* of homosexuals in a bar was considered "disorderly" by the police, who could force the bar to close. For the next thirty years, homosexuals in states such as New York would be legally prohibited from openly socializing or working where liquor was being sold.

Interestingly, this new prohibition encouraged some bars to cater *exclusively* to homosexuals, which until then had been a fairly rare phenomenon. Because homosexuals were barred from going to regular bars, a demand developed for gay bars. Shady bars that wanted to cash in on that business often had to pay off local police to stay open, and organized crime syndicates that had sold bootleg liquor during Prohibition had the required connections. Because gays and lesbians had no other options at the time, these new Mafia-run bars catering just to homosexuals could charge higher prices and mistreat their customers as much as they liked. Without any meaningful competition, these bars didn't put much effort into creating a nice environment—anyway, they usually only stayed open for short periods of time.

It's important to remember that at this time, people who were attracted to others of the same sex usually had nowhere to hang out together except at these illicit bars. There were no organizations or clubs exclusively for them and, of course, no Web sites or online chat rooms. There simply was nowhere public and safe where lesbians and gays could meet and be themselves together.

Hard Times

ABOVE: Unemployed men outside a Depression soup kitchen. Chicago, Illinois, February 1931.

OPPOSITE: *The Fleet's In!* by artist Paul Cadmus. 1934. The man speaking to the sailors wears a signal red tie.

THE ECONOMIC EFFECTS of the Great Depression made it hard for women who wanted to support themselves, so life became *especially* difficult for lesbians. Men were losing their jobs at an alarming rate (by 1933, the unemployment rate was around 25 percent), and women were increasingly expected to give up their jobs so that men could have them. Women who chose to remain at work were often vilified as being selfish, since they were supposedly keeping a man from providing for his family. Even the dean of a top women's college told a graduating group of students in the early 1930s, "Perhaps the greatest service that you can render to the community . . . is to have the courage to refuse to work for gain." Some states even passed laws forcing women to quit teaching jobs once they got married.

Historian George Chauncey has argued that the loss of so many men's jobs created a national

sense of gender insecurity, in which men didn't feel like they were really men. This led to such things as public artwork that glorified idealized, muscular male laborers, and the widespread criticism of working women. Homosexuality was therefore extra-offensive because it did not follow traditional gender roles—even discussing the subject seemed dangerous. Many of the advances toward visibility made by homosexuals up to this point—drag balls, pansy acts, known gay hot spots, representations of homosexuality in the arts—would be buried during this decade by police action, medical opinion, and an absence of homosexuality in the public eye. One lesbian remembered those difficult years, saying "there was no question of coming out. I wanted so much to be able to talk freely with people, to be like everyone else, not to feel like we loved in a wasteland, but that was impossible. I had a lot of heterosexual women friends, but I thought that as long as I was in that relationship I could never have a close friend. I knew how much people would have looked down on us if they'd guessed." For many lesbian women in the upper and middle class, marriage seemed to be their only option, both for social and economic reasons. Writer Samuel Steward recalled gay life in the Depression years as "very secretive. Everybody was in the closet. There were no marches, no organizations, nothing like that. We lived under an umbrella of ignorance."

Yet, despite the odds, the homosexual life that had blossomed in the 1920s was not destroyed. A hidden subculture continued in the nation's largest cities, where men began using the term "gay" to describe themselves, a use of the term that would not be clear to the rest of the population for several decades. ("Gay" had originally meant "care-free," but the term began to refer to immoral pleasures in the 1600s, and in the nineteenth century applied to female prostitutes. However, most people continued to use the word in its original meaning, and homosexual camp culture embraced the term as a code word.) These men developed a constantly changing system of signals to recognize each other in public places—at different times they bleached their hair, added bright feathers to their hat bands, put on red ties or green suits, wore dark brown or gray suede shoes, plucked their eyebrows, or dropped hints in conversation, an activity called "dropping hairpins." Known "cruising" areas (places where men gathered for sexual encounters) persisted in big cities and small towns alike, despite the threat of police action. Gay bars continued to operate in New York and elsewhere, and there were also lesbian bars in New York, Buffalo, Cleveland, Detroit, Oakland, San Francisco, Chicago, and other cities. For Samuel Steward and others, the need for secrecy was exciting: "We had to be very careful in those days, but in the end I think we had more fun."

Internal Affairs at the White House

IRONICALLY, in a decade of gay and lesbian invisibility, one of the most visible women in America was carrying on a lesbian affair. President Franklin D. Roosevelt wasn't the most faithfully married man, and, as it turns out, his wife, Eleanor, wasn't that committed to fidelity, either. Historian Blanche Wiesen Cook has argued that not only did Eleanor Roosevelt carry on an affair with a younger man named Earl Miller, she also had an affair with a successful political reporter named Lorena Hickok. The two women met when Hickok was assigned to report on Eleanor during the 1932 presidential campaign, and the two grew intimate. Hickok quit journalism to work for the Roosevelt administration, and she eventually moved to the White House in 1941—though the evidence we have left today indicates that Roosevelt's romantic interest had cooled somewhat by then. Nevertheless, they remained close until Roosevelt's death in 1962.

Some historians have tried to write off their relationship as a chaste, Victorian-style one, but as Wiesen Cook pointed out, "ER and Hick were not involved in a schoolgirl 'smash.' They did not meet in a nineteenth-century storybook, or swoon unrequitedly on a nineteenth-century campus." Roosevelt was very aware of lesbian life—in fact, her closest friends during the 1920s were two lesbian couples. The surviving record of Roosevelt and Hickok's intimacy is abundant—the Franklin D. Roosevelt Library in Hyde Park, New York, has 2,336 letters from Roosevelt to Hickok, and another 1,024 from Hickok to Roosevelt. However, those letters are just part of the letters that were actually written—Wiesen Cook recounts that after Roosevelt's death, Hickok and Esther Lape, one of Roosevelt's lesbian friends, "sat around an open fire at Lape's Connecticut estate and spent hours burning letter after letter." Likewise, after Hickok's death, her sister destroyed another group of letters she found in Hickok's home. Even still, Wiesen Cook concludes, "For all the deletions and restraint, the thousands of letters that remain are amorous and specific."

Here's a quick sampling:

MARCH 7, 1933 (*to Hickok*): "Hick darling . . . Oh, I want to put my arms around you. I ache to hold you close. Your ring is a great comfort, I look at it and think she does love me or else I wouldn't be wearing it."

MARCH 9, 1933 (*to Hickok*): "My pictures are nearly all up and I have you in my sitting room where I can look at you most of my waking hours! I can't kiss you so I kiss your picture good night and good morning!"

DECEMBER 5, 1933 (*to Roosevelt*): "I've been trying today to bring back your face—to remember just how you look . . . Most clearly I remember your eyes with a kind of teasing smile in them, and the feeling of that soft spot just northeast of the corner of your mouth against my lips. . . ."

SEPTEMBER 1, 1934 (*to Hickok*): "I wish I could lie down beside you tonight and take you in my arms."

Eleanor Roosevelt dining with Lorena Hickok. August 1, 1934.

"Persons with homosexual histories are to be found in every age group, in every social level, in every conceivable occupation, in cities and on farms, and in the most remote areas of the country."

—DR. ALFRED KINSEY, *SEXUAL BEHAVIOR IN THE HUMAN MALE*, 1948

3 LET'S GET TOGETHER
1940–1959

Los Angeles, 1947

CLICK. CLACK. CLACKETY. Click clack. Click. Ding!

A few more rows to go, and the issue would be finished. *Well, at least my typing's getting faster,* thought Lisa with a smile. This was the second time she had typed out the entire magazine—but there would be ten copies in total, since she typed five sheets at a time using carbon paper.

Click Click. Clack.

Another issue of *Vice Versa*, hot off the presses! She'll take the issues along tonight and pass them out at the If Club—it was a great icebreaker.

Clack. Clackety. Click clack.

Lisa had moved down to Los Angeles from upstate two years ago, and she discovered that making friends was pretty tough. Truth be told, she was lonely a great deal, living all by herself in the city.

Clack. Clack.

Oh, it was all right. It was better than living back upstate, where Lisa's overbearing mother was always coming by and going through her things.

In any case, it wasn't long before Lisa met the girls.

Click. Click clack. Ding!

Lisa smiled as she remembered it: There they all were, lying on the roof of the garage sunning themselves, talking. Then one of the girls asked Lisa, "Are you gay?" Lisa thought for a moment. "Well, I try to be as happy as I can under the circumstances." Oh, they had laughed about that. Lisa had never heard that use of the word "gay" (nor had she ever heard the word "lesbian," for that matter). When the girls explained what the word meant, Lisa answered, "Well, yes, I guess I am because I don't really go out and search for boyfriends. I don't care for that." They invited Lisa along to a softball game, and Lisa agreed—even though softball bored the tar out of her.

Clack click. Click. Click.

And the next week they took her to the If Club for the first time.

Ding!

The air was thick with smoke. Many of the gay gals inside had close-cropped hair and tailored clothes. But it wasn't just girls inside—on the other side of the club there was a bar where men sat and watched the girls dance. Lisa figured they were straight, but couldn't be sure. She later learned that the proprietor wouldn't let the men go to the girls' side.

In one of the booths, a bunch of gals were singing "Happy Birthday" while a cake was brought out to them. Lisa thought, *How wonderful that all these girls can be together.* Then she realized she had tears in her eyes.

It wasn't long before someone came up to Lisa and asked her to dance. Lisa looked feminine, with her jewelry and long, wavy brown hair. Lisa said yes. She would say yes to a lot of dances in the coming months.

Click clack. Clack.

Lisa got to know different people at the club. Sometimes she would be invited to other bars, like that one down at the beach. She loved going to these places, but it still made her nervous. The police could barge in at any time, even though they tended to pick on the boys' gay clubs. Lisa was careful not to drink—she didn't want to be drunk if the police *did* show up—so she always ordered Coke or 7-Up or something like that. She had never been in a real raid, but the last time Lisa was at the beach bar, the police had come in and swaggered around. They surrounded one boy in a red shirt. Then they made him "prove" he was a boy—*What a horrible thing to do to the poor fellow*, thought Lisa, steamed. Before they left, the police came around and took everyone's names—Lisa was sure to mumble her name quietly, so the policeman wouldn't really catch it. He didn't seem to think she was gay, with her earrings and long hair, so he moved on. Lisa never went back to that place.

Clack. Ding! Click click.

During the day, Lisa worked as a secretary at the offices of the RKO movie studio. Her boss was nice enough—he told her straight off that she wouldn't have a lot to do. But Lisa should always look busy, he said. So earlier this summer, she came up with the idea to start a magazine that she could type in her small office.

Clack clack. Click.

Lisa had named it *Vice Versa*, "America's Gayest Magazine." She just passed issues out for free at the bar and told people, "When you get through this, don't throw it away, pass it on to another gay gal." She used to mail them out, too (with no return address, and she certainly didn't put her real name on the magazine!),

"Lisa Ben," founder of *Vice Versa*.

but then a friend called to tell her to stop. "It's against the law," she said, "you could get yourself in big trouble."

Lisa wrote almost everything in the magazine—poetry, essays, reviews of movies and books. This issue had a review of Radclyffe Hall's *The Well of Loneliness*. OK, the book was published twenty years ago, but there weren't a lot of relevant books being published in those days. And the movies weren't really gay movies, they just had plots with close relationships between women. But the magazine was fun to do, and it was a great way to meet people.

Click clack. Ding!

Vice Versa—Lisa really liked the name. It meant "the opposite." *Everyone considers our kind of life a vice—but it's actually just the opposite!* she thought, still smiling.

Lisa pulled the sheets out of the typewriter, shuffled them together into a neat pile, and put them into her bag. She checked her lipstick in her palm mirror, shut off the lights, and closed the door to the office. She walked confidently down the hall, humming quietly to herself.

"ISA BEN" CREATED ONLY NINE ISSUES of *Vice Versa*; the Valentine's Day issue of 1948 was the last. RKO was bought by another company, and a lot of people were laid off, including Lisa. At her next job, she didn't have as much time or privacy—and there would definitely be trouble if her magazine were discovered.

But times were changing. World War II had transformed America in many ways, and there were growing communities of gays and lesbians in the country's biggest cities. Lisa's magazine was proof that gays and lesbians were beginning to think about themselves as a group more and more.

Maybe it was finally time for homosexuals to get organized. . . .

Make Love

THERE ARE A LOT OF THINGS people remember about World War II, such as the difficulties of wartime food rationing, the shameful internment of Japanese Americans in the United States, the horrific genocide of Jews (as well as gay men and other groups) in Europe, the hard-won victory over the Nazi forces in Germany, and the controversial deployment of the atomic bomb in Japan. But we don't often hear about how World War II was also responsible for a whole lot of *sex*. Military men, military women, civilians—they were all getting together like they never had before. As one wartime teenager later described it, life was "a real sex paradise." Millions of people entered the military, and millions more moved to different states during the war, away from the prying eyes of

Two women sit on the laps of two uniformed men and kiss them in the card room of a residence for women war workers. Arlington, Virginia, June 1943.

their families and neighbors. And with grim news coming from Europe and the Pacific, life never seemed so short. Naturally, folks wanted to take advantage of it. Playwright Arthur Laurents recalled, "*Everybody* did it—in numbers."

Indeed, it wasn't just straights who were getting some. World War II was what historian John D'Emilio called "a nation-wide 'coming out' experience." In new cities, at new defense department jobs, homosexual women and men from every corner of the country were suddenly able to access a previously unimaginable, underground gay culture. Writer Gore Vidal recalled, "Everybody was released by the war; people were doing things they hadn't dreamed of in the villages from whence they came. Under the right circumstances, everyone was available." One gay man later remembered how soldiers like him "sort of did with their gay behavior what they did with everything else. Which was take chances and risks and try to enjoy things because who knows where you might be sent tomorrow." After the dark years of the 1930s, gay nightlife began to pick up some: gay bars opened in Denver, Chicago, San Jose, Cleveland, San Francisco, Kansas City, Los Angeles, and other cities to take advantage of the more relaxed social atmosphere during the war.

Uncle Sam Wants YOU

BEFORE WORLD WAR II, the military didn't spend a lot of time worrying about homosexuals joining up. But by 1942, psychiatrists had managed to convince the Department of Defense to start screening the psychiatric as well as physical health of all potential soldiers (remember, homosexuality was considered a mental illness in those days). Psychiatrists put together guidelines for recruiters to identify homosexuals during the screening process. As a *Newsweek* article explained, those guidelines instructed screeners to look for homosexuals' "effeminate looks and behavior and by repeating certain words from the homosexual vocabulary and watching for signs of recognition." Well, they didn't do a great job:

less than five thousand men were excluded for homosexuality out of the eighteen million men screened. (No records were kept about how many lesbians were denied from serving.)

Many gay men found the induction screening to be a joke. It wasn't hard for most to pass as straight, and recruiters often didn't push the issue. A gay man named Bob Ruffing enlisted in the navy, and he later remembered how he "walked into this office, and here was this man who was a screaming belle—lots of gold braid but he was a queen if I ever saw one. And he asked me the standard questions, ending with, 'Did you ever have any homosexual experiences?' Well, I looked him right in the eye and said, 'No.' And he looked right back and said, 'That's good.' Both of us lying through our teeth!" As historian Allan Bérubé has pointed out, it was ironic that for many young men this "mass sexual questioning" was "the first time that they had to think of their lives in homosexual terms"— in other words, the military was systematically presenting the *possibility* of homosexuality to millions of people. So much for the silence of the 1930s!

Man the Guns—Join the Navy recruitment poster by McClelland Barclay. 1942.

G.I. Janes

MEN WEREN'T THE ONLY ONES ANSWERING Uncle Sam's call: almost a third of a million women served in the armed forces during World War II, with nearly 150,000 joining the largest women's branch, the Women's Army Corps (WACs). Other branches included Women Marines, Women's Army Air Corps, the WAVES, and the Coast Guard SPARS. The all-female environment of these branches of the military included a high percentage of lesbians—historian Lillian Faderman compared the situation to women's colleges; these women "worked together in pursuits they could consider important, and where they could become heroes to one another without the constant distraction of male measuring sticks. It is not surprising that many of them discovered through their military experiences that they wanted to be lesbians. And there was not much to discourage them." While the psychological screening process tried to flag men who were not "masculine," the psych exam for women actually favored masculine qualities, since the armed forces needed women who could do "masculine" work.

Join the WAAC recruitment poster. Circa 1939–1945.

The Boys at War

THE MILITARY EXPERIENCE was in some ways positive for many gay men because they were able to travel and see the world. One veteran nostalgically remembered how he felt walking into a gay club in Paris, when "suddenly you realized the size of homosexuality—the total global reach of it! There were hundreds of guys from all over the world in all kinds of uniforms: there were free Poles dancing with American soldiers; there were Scotsmen dancing with Algerians; there were Free French; there were Russians. It was like a U.N. of gays. It was just incredible. I mean there were men dancing with each other! I had never seen that before in my *life!*"

To entertain the troops, the military set up all-male theatrical productions, including several productions of Clare Boothe Luce's notoriously campy *The Women*. Playwright Arthur Laurents remembered seeing a performance as a soldier at Fort Aberdeen, Maryland: "it was really like Alice in Wonderland down the rabbit hole, I could not believe any of this. They did *The Women* with all these guys and they had bras and they walked around in underwear and they had the big scene with Crystal in the bathtub. She stood up and had a jockstrap on. But it was done straight. . . . It never occurred to me that they would do anything like that. God! The army was a strange place."

Some units were more open to gay men than others. One gay man later recounted how he joined the volunteer ambulance corps (American Field Service), and found himself in the front lines in Egypt "sleeping in a foxhole in the desert with fleas and rats." There were several other gay men in his unit, and he remembered how he and his friends found comfort in their flamboyance. "We used to call Hitler 'Helen.' And we'd be in the desert, and there'd be a lot of German planes, and we'd say, 'Helen's angry today. God, she's mad.'"

But life in the army certainly wasn't fun and games, even if you were able to connect with gay peers. Battle was brutal and deadly, and many gay men lost their loved ones in combat. The need for secrecy only amplified their grief. One aircorpsman recalled witnessing his lover's death: "His plane blew up in front of my face. . . . You never really get over something like that. And you know, something happened. I stopped living for a while. And I couldn't grieve, because I'd be a punk if I grieved, and be treated like those men in the blue outfits." "Punk" was slang for gay men, and black soldiers found guilty of homosexuality were forced to wear blue uniforms and suffered terrible public indignities and threats of violence. The military segregated black and white soldiers during World War II; they would be formally integrated in units together throughout the armed services by a presidential order in 1948.

But stories of kindheartedness survive, too. When soldier Ben Small's boyfriend died in a bombing attack, he "went into a three-day period of hysterics." Small remembered, "I was treated with such kindness by the guys I worked with, who were all totally aware of why I had gone hysterical. . . . And one guy in the tent came up to me, and said, 'Why didn't you tell me you were gay? You could have talked to me.' This big, straight, macho guy. There was a sort of compassion then."

Ready, Set, DISCHARGE!

HOMOSEXUALITY THEN (as now) was grounds for discharge from the military. During World War II, those discharges were technically neither honorable nor dishonorable, although they declared the individual to be "undesirable." If you got a "blue discharge," as they were sometimes called for being printed on blue paper, you didn't qualify for the fat package of rights and benefits that other veterans received, and it often made it much harder to get a job. From 1941 to 1945, about nine thousand people, mostly men, got those blue discharges. That's quite a lot, considering that in the forty years leading up to the war, only a few hundred people in the military were convicted of sodomy. Then again, instead of being discharged, those convicted earlier had been sentenced to prison.

During World War II, the military often turned a blind eye toward homosexuality because it needed as much troop power as it could get. Sgt. Johnnie Phelps worked for Gen. Dwight D. Eisenhower during the war in a WAC battalion, and fifty years later she recalled a time when the general had ordered her to find and "get rid" of all the lesbians:

ABOVE: Portrait of Johnnie Phelps, WAC sergeant during World War II.

OPPOSITE: Cover of *Billy Budd, Sailor* by Herman Melville. Homosexuality is one of the themes that figure prominently in the book.

I said, "Well, sir, if the general pleases, sir, I'd be happy to do this investigation for you. But you have to know that the first name on the list will be mine."

And he was kind of taken aback a bit. . . . I looked at him, and I said, "Sir, you're right. They're lesbians in the WAC battalion. And if the general is prepared to replace all the file clerks, all the section commanders, all of the drivers—every woman in the WAC detachment—and there were about nine hundred and eighty something of us—then I'll be happy to make that list. But I think the general should be aware that among those women are the most highly decorated women in the war. There have been no cases of illegal pregnancies. There have been no cases of AWOL. There have been no cases of misconduct. And as a matter of fact, every six months since we've been here, sir, the general has awarded us a commendation for meritorious service."

And he said, "Forget the order."

In 1944, the Inspector General's office started an investigation of homosexuality at Women's Army Corps training center in Fort Oglethorpe, Georgia, after someone's mother filed a complaint. Despite finding all kinds of evidence, the investigators stubbornly declared they couldn't find any "homosexual addicts" and recommended that no further investigations be conducted for the duration of the war.

Here, Witchy Witchy Witchy . . .

ONCE THE WAR ENDED, though, all bets were off. The military started aggressive investigations that terrified homosexual servicepeople stationed all over the world. Pat Bond was a WAC serving in Japan. She remembered, "They started an incredible witch hunt in Tokyo. Unbelievable. Sending five hundred women home for dishonorable discharges. Every day there were courts-martial and trials—you were there testifying against your friends, or they were testifying against you . . . until you got afraid to look your neighbor in the eye. Afraid of everything." The military arranged "queer ships" to send identified homosexuals with "undesirable" discharges back to the nearest U.S. port. Many of those men and women knew they wouldn't be welcome at home, so they stayed in cities like New York, San Francisco, Los Angeles, and Boston. In the late 1940s, the armed forces discharged about a thousand homosexuals every year. That number doubled by the early 1950s.

On the bright side, this huge influx of gays and lesbians into those cities gave new strength and life to the homosexual communities already found there. A group of war veterans in New York started up one of the earliest gay social organizations in America, the Veterans Benevolent Association, in 1945. The group was largely social, hosting dances, campy cross-dressing socials, guest speakers, and even a "Stitch and Bitch" sewing group. A few of the veterans had wives, and oddly enough, one of those wives was a founder of the gay group that did most of the work keeping the group together until 1954. One veteran recalled, "The women were all straight, but they knew their husbands were gay and they just went along with the husbands." But the postwar era grew increasingly hostile toward homosexuals; in later years, the Veterans Benevolent Association began excluding effeminate men in order to keep a lower profile.

Gay Lit 101

SOME SAY A SO-CALLED gay sensibility in American literature can be traced back to the nineteenth century, particularly in Herman Melville's suggestive descriptions of relationships between sailors. However, the homosexual subculture that began flourishing in big cities during World War II really took male homosexuality in literature to a new level. Several novels about gay life were published in the postwar period, including Gore Vidal's *The City and the Pillar* in 1948, which gave mainstream Americans a glimpse into the homosexual underworld of cities like Los Angeles and New Orleans.

ENRICHED CLASSIC

BILLY BUDD, SAILOR
HERMAN MELVILLE

Includes detailed explanatory notes, an overview of key themes, and more

It was an open secret that the best-known playwright of the 1940s and 1950s, Tennessee Williams, was gay. In fact, a few of his early one-act plays were explicitly gay, though almost all of his later, more mainstream work featured heterosexual characters (as in *The Glass Menagerie* and *A Streetcar Named Desire*). Nevertheless, critics recognized that Williams's plays reflected his own conflicted views on homosexuality, and some critics even argued that he merely disguised gay characters as straight.

Truman Capote was another successful writer who played up his gay public persona. His work included novels such as *Other Voices, Other Rooms* (1948) and *Breakfast at Tiffany's* (1958), as well as the nonfiction classic, *In Cold Blood* (1965). As one literary historian noted, Capote's work "helped establish what might be called the quintessential homosexual writing style of the 1950s and 1960s, with clear links to the writing of Tennessee Williams. . . . That style was at once closeted, in that it seldom dealt with overt homosexuality, and uncloseted, because its code for homosexual interpretations was so easily seen through."

James Baldwin wrote several works, including *Go Tell It on the Mountain* (1953) and *Another Country* (1962), about the complexities of being both homosexual and African American in a hostile culture. His second novel, *Giovanni's Room* (1956), included an early spirited defense of homosexuality.

TOP: Truman Capote, shortly after the publication of his first novel, *Other Voices, Other Rooms*. 1948.

BOTTOM: James Baldwin, novelist and essayist. Circa 1950s.

OPPOSITE: Portrait of American scientist and researcher Dr. Alfred Kinsey. July 1948.

Sex Ed

IN 1948, a fifty-three-year-old Indiana zoologist named Dr. Alfred Kinsey (whose specialty was the gall wasp) published a scientific work with a pretty uninspiring title, *Sexual Behavior in the Human Male*, and a follow-up book in 1953 called *Sexual Behavior in the Human Female*. In these two eight-hundred-plus-page books, Kinsey presented and analyzed the results of an intense study of the sexual practices of twelve thousand white American men and women. While earlier sexologists had focused on what were then considered sexual "abnormalities," no major scientific survey had ever been conducted on what most Americans were actually *doing*, sexually speaking.

Kinsey's results were surprising—in fact, shocking. Masturbation among men was found to be almost universal. Half of married men were sexually unfaithful, as well as a quarter of married women. Half of the surveyed men had admitted to same-sex attraction, a whopping 37 percent had had homosexual experiences leading to orgasm, and 4 percent were exclusively homosexual. Among women, 28 percent had experienced homosexual attraction, and 13 percent had followed through. Kinsey's results led him to develop his famous 0–6 scale as a way to categorize people's desires along a range that spanned from purely heterosexual (rating 0) to purely homosexual (rating 6).

The books were not intended to be sensational, but America was stunned. Initially, the first book's publisher had called for a printing of 5,000 copies, but within weeks the number was boosted to 185,000. The books were major best sellers—people everywhere were talking about Kinsey's project. In 1948 and 1949, academics organized more than two hundred conferences to discuss the subject. Kinsey became a household name, and his face was plastered on the cover of *Time* magazine. Of course, a lot of people were upset—one university president described Kinsey's work as being like "the work of small boys writing dirty words on fences," and a Congressional committee threatened to investigate him for trying to destroy American morality. Psychiatrists in particular were peeved— as historian Charles Kaiser pointed out, "Kinsey had implied that the entire psychiatric profession was guilty of massive medical malpractice." Kinsey's methods and conclusions would be debated for decades to come. Nevertheless, his books and the notoriety they received finally made sex an acceptable topic of discussion for the mainstream American public—a public suddenly aware of how extensive homosexuality was.

The Homosexual Threat

THE FLIP SIDE of discovering how common homosexual acts really were among Americans was that it fed into a growing sense of national paranoia. Suspense films like Hitchcock's *Suspicion* and *Spellbound* had put a sinister spin on what wives across America were experiencing: the men who came back from the war were different from the husbands who had left. After World War II ended in 1945, America found itself in the midst of another war, the Cold War, in which the threat of nuclear weapons played on people's worst fears. Although the Axis powers had been defeated, the Soviet Union, China, and a growing number of other Communist nations quickly became seen as new competitors and enemies of American-style democracy. Their dictatorial, oppressive government regimes caused Americans to fear Communism, a political philosophy that encouraged militant workers' revolutions to overthrow governments in order to establish an idealized, classless society. Senator Joseph McCarthy claimed (lied, really) that Communists were infiltrating the government, thereby sparking a whole series of Congressional investigations on a host of conspiracy allegations.

Illogically, homosexuals were also roped into hysteria about Communists—gays and lesbians were considered dangerous not only because of their supposed predatory "perversion" or "deviant" behavior, but also because they were thought to be vulnerable to blackmail. Throughout American culture there was also a return to traditional gender roles as soldiers returned to their families after the war. Middle-class women were expected to marry and become housewives (think of those old black-and-white TV sitcoms, like *Leave It to Beaver* and *The Donna Reed Show*, in which women were idealized for their effortless housekeeping).

Suspense...
that mounts with every embrace!

A story of love ...under the threat of MURDER!

CARY GRANT
JOAN FONTAINE
in
Suspicion!
Directed by ALFRED HITCHCOCK
with · SIR CEDRIC HARDWICKE · NIGEL BRUCE · DAME MAY WHITTY
Screenplay by SAMSON RAPHAELSON, JOAN HARRISON and ALMA REVILLE

Traditional-role-defying homosexuals were in a bad spot. The 1950s would, in a lot of ways, be a reprise of the 1930s for gays and lesbians—another dark decade.

Beginning in 1947, President Harry S. Truman's National Security Loyalty Program instructed the State Department to fire suspected homosexuals as security risks. In addition, Nebraska Senator Kenneth Wherry took a leading role in identifying homosexuals in government: the subcommittee he cochaired concluded in 1950 that every homosexual had "a corrosive influence upon his fellow employees. These perverts will frequently attempt to entice normal individuals to engage in perverted practices. . . . One homosexual can pollute a Government Office." Kinsey's statistics were even quoted and manipulated as "proof" of homosexuality's reach in government by sensationalizing journalists. Sadly, President Eisenhower, who as the top general during World War II had canceled his own order to identify and remove lesbians in a WAC battalion, took the craziness one step

ABOVE: Senator Joseph McCarthy (left) and Senator Kenneth Wherry. 1950.

OPPOSITE: Advertising poster for the classic American film *Suspicion*, starring Cary Grant and Joan Fontaine and directed by Alfred Hitchcock. 1941.

further by issuing Executive Order 10405 in 1953 to ban employment of homosexuals in the federal government. It wasn't long before state and local governments followed suit. (Meanwhile, a 1957 navy study known as the Crittenden Report concluded that there was no evidence that homosexuals serving in the military posed more of a security risk than heterosexuals.)

The witch-hunt mentality was contagious. In 1955, the city of Boise, Idaho, was seized with panic after three men were arrested and charged with having sex with underage boys—the police warned of the existence of a "homosexual ring." Nearly 1,500 citizens were questioned, lists of suspected homosexuals were compiled, and sixteen men were arrested. Ten of them were sent to the penitentiary—some for just having consensual sex with another adult. Understandably, many terrified gay men fled the city to avoid being drawn into the scandal.

The Mattachine Candidate

N THE LATE 1940s, a man named Harry Hay taught a music history course at the People's Educational Center in Los Angeles. Hay had been a dedicated Communist Party organizer for many years, and he had been active in the gay communities of San Francisco and Los Angeles before coming out to his party superiors in 1938—they told him to marry instead, which he did. Nevertheless, ten years later, Hay found himself at a gay party one night, where he and a group of men joked about forming a gay "Bachelors for Wallace" campaign in support of the Progressive Party's presidential nominee, Henry Wallace. (Wallace was widely viewed as a pro-Communist candidate.) No one took the idea seriously, but Hay was intrigued by the idea of using his Communist Party organizing techniques to mobilize homosexuals to demand rights. He sounded out some of his ideas with heterosexual friends in progressive organizations, but could see that he wasn't getting anywhere. He decided that homosexuals had to do it for themselves.

In 1950, Hay nervously approached one of his students, Bob Hull, with his idea, suspecting that Hull might be homosexual. He was relieved to learn that Hull was indeed gay, as was his roommate, Chuck Rowland, and they both had experience with the Communist Party. The three had many discussions about the idea, and Hay soon included a dancer and fashion designer named Rudi Gernreich and Dale Jennings, a writer who had been active defending the civil liberties of Japanese Americans during the war. These five men formed the Mattachine Society.

Chuck Rowland with Konrad Stevens, Dale Jennings, Harry Hay, Rudy Gernreich, Stan Witt, Bob Hull, and Paul Bernard at a Mattachine Society Christmas party. Los Angeles, 1951 or 1952.

Hay later explained that the name "Mattachine" came from a medieval group of French bachelors who held dances and rituals where they would perform in masks. Hay saw a connection between those "masked people, unknown and anonymous" and the homosexuals of his day. The society he helped put together was itself very secretive—with all their experience with the Communist Party, the founders were used to hiding from the government. (They weren't being paranoid; years later it was discovered that the FBI *had* been monitoring Mattachine meetings.) The original founders modeled the organization on the Communist Party's cell structure by instituting five "orders," or levels, of membership, the fifth order being the founders. In the early Mattachine days, members often had no clue about who was running the organization—or even the meetings. They were aware only of the members of their own order, until they were promoted up to higher levels. The founders figured that the less people knew about the structure and leadership of the organization, the better the chances of the organization surviving a police raid.

The Mattachine Society held semipublic discussion groups to talk about basic questions: What caused homosexuality? Why was it viewed so negatively? Could homosexuals lead happy, contented lives? How could they improve the public's view of homosexuality? Many people who came to these meetings, including the leadership, used fake names—most were terrified, thinking that government agents would storm in at any minute. But when nothing happened over time, the members relaxed. These men and women (though mostly men) formed close friendships as they shared their personal experiences, often for the first time. They began to think about themselves differently, as an oppressed minority.

The new organization grew in numbers, and Hay decided it was time to end his ties with the Communist Party and focus his efforts on the Mattachine Society. He also realized, however late, that it was high time he ended his thirteen-year marriage.

The first major challenge for the Mattachine Society was fighting a criminal charge against Dale Jennings for "lewd and dissolute behavior." The organization saw it as a plain case of police entrapment. It was a common problem that undercover police would try to get gay men to approach them in order to make an arrest. In February 1952, a plainclothes vice squad officer made sexual advances on Jennings at a park and followed him home to arrest him. The society distributed leaflets in bars, beaches, and various cruising spots around the city publicizing the case and seeking contributions for Jennings's defense. Hay later remembered that even some gay supermarket clerks helped by slipping flyers into shoppers' bags. After the jury deadlocked and the district attorney's office decided to drop the charges, Mattachine declared a victory—and the membership grew. By 1953, the organization had about two thousand members and almost a hundred discussion groups. Soon the organization spread to the San Francisco area, where greater numbers of women participated.

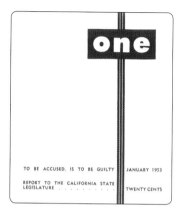

One of the discussion groups in Los Angeles decided to start *ONE*, the first openly gay national publication in the United States. (Though closely related, *ONE* was technically separate from the Mattachine Society.) The letters to the editor in early issues show that many more people all over the country were reading the magazine than the two-thousand-some subscribers.

Hooker to the Rescue

DESPITE THE QUESTIONS that Kinsey's work brought up, gays and lesbians were still considered to be sick and maladjusted by the mental health profession. At some clinics, "treatments" still included such horrors as castration, lobotomy, and electroshock therapy.

One of the early members of the Mattachine Society was a former psychology student named "Sammy." Sammy had taken a course taught by Dr. Evelyn Hooker at the University of California in Los Angeles, and afterward he befriended her and her husband. After Sammy and his partner took Hooker and her husband to Finocchio's, a well-known female-impersonator club, they begged Dr. Hooker to do a scientific study on homosexuals. Sammy knew he and his friends were well-adjusted, and he believed Dr. Hooker could prove it. She was reluctant at first but was convinced in time after one of her colleagues insisted it would be valuable research.

In 1953, Hooker received a grant from the National Institute of Mental Health and began her work. She gathered thirty homosexual volunteers through the Mattachine Society and gave each of them three psychological tests. Then she found thirty heterosexual male volunteers (which was harder than she had expected) and gave them the same tests. Psychologists believed they could rate psychological

TOP: Cover of first issue of *ONE*. January 1953.

BOTTOM: Dr. Evelyn Hooker. Circa 1950s.

OPPOSITE: Cover of *The Homosexual in America: A Subjective Approach* by Donald Webster Cory, first published in 1951.

health from these tests. After *both* groups rated the same score of average or better, Hooker knew her work showed for the first time that homosexuality was not a psychological illness per se. In 1956, she presented her results in a paper, "The Adjustment of the Male Overt Homosexual," to the American Psychological Association (APA) conference in Chicago. Hooker's work was important in stopping the most extreme treatments for homosexuality. Hooker later remembered how people would often approach her and thank her, for they had been spared torture at clinics because of her research.

Unfortunately, Sammy never got to see the results of the study—he died in a car crash before it was released. In any case, another twenty years would pass before the American Psychiatric Association would consider taking homosexuality off its list of disorders.

A Call to Arms

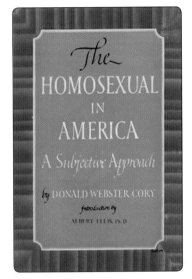

IN 1951, an important book hit the scene, *The Homosexual in America: A Subjective Approach* by Donald Webster Cory. Actually, "Donald Webster Cory" was a fake name—the author was really Edward Sagarin, a Brooklyn man who had a wife and son. Sagarin's family didn't know anything about his boyfriend—or his book, which went to press seven times between 1951 and 1957. The book described the difficulties of gay men's lives, and suggested how American attitudes might be changed. He lamented, "Tolerance is the ugliest word in our language. . . . I can't see why anyone should be struggling to be tolerated. If people are not good, they should not be tolerated, and if they are good, they should be *accepted.*"

For thousands of gay men and women, this book was important in changing the way they viewed themselves, as well as how they viewed the possibilities ahead. Sagarin wistfully declared, "If only all of the inverts, the millions in all lands, could simultaneously rise up in our full strength!"

The Homophile Coup

BUT IN MARCH 1953, the height of the McCarthy anti-Communist hysteria, very few would dare even dream what Cory and the Mattachine founders envisioned. Instead, the Communist past of several of Mattachine's founders became a huge problem. A Los Angeles columnist wrote an article suggesting the group could be infiltrated and used for dangerous, Communist purposes. The journalist pointed out that the group's legal adviser, Fred Snider, had recently refused to answer questions in front of the House Un-American Activities Committee. After reading the article, several vocal Mattachine members started questioning the secrecy of the organization and especially the identities of the leadership—they thought the columnist had brought up some good concerns. The pressure mounted, and the founders decided to call an open democratic conference of delegates in April to rework the society's constitution. Within months, the organization was taken over by a group of people with very different ideas, and the embittered founders left the organization.

The new leadership of the Mattachine group ushered in the "homophile" period of the gay rights movement. For the next ten years, gay organizations would focus largely on integrating into mainstream society and denying their differences in order to gain acceptance—not, as the Mattachine founders had envisioned, to recognize homosexuals as a minority group with its own culture that should demand equal treatment.

The Mattachine Society would now attempt to educate and get the support of "experts," in the hopes that those experts would embrace homosexuals and become their defenders in the public sphere. Hall Call, the new president, later explained, "To be just an organization of upstart gays, we would have been shattered and ridiculed and put down." Unfortunately, the new strategy never produced much fruit—even Dr. Hooker and Dr. Kinsey encouraged the group not to think of themselves as a minority group. The Mattachine discussion groups went from being inspiring, consciousness-raising political sessions to being little more than therapy groups, discussing individual problems. Within months of the leadership change, Mattachine's membership rolls started shrinking, and the organization—though it would remain the largest homosexual organization for a long time—would never again be as radical or as popular as it was at its beginnings.

ONE magazine (now run by ONE, Inc.), however, took advantage of its independence from the Mattachine Society and continued to promote the founders' vision of homosexuals as an oppressed minority—Dale Jennings continued to work on the magazine after Call took over the society. Jim Kepner wrote a column for the magazine, reporting on bar raids, censorship, and various entrapment arrests that helped raise gay men's awareness of the extent of their situation across America. He later remembered, "I got lots of complaints about the column from readers because the news was bad. . . . I explained several times to *ONE* subscribers that…I depended on the straight press, and those were the kinds of stories they were publishing about gays." (Although in one notable exception, Chicago's black press gave extensive, largely positive coverage during the 1950s to elaborate annual drag balls held on the city's South Side, which drew both gay and straight spectators.)

The postmaster in Los Angeles seized the August 1953 issue of *ONE*, but soon released it. Then, in 1954, the post office seized the October issue, claiming it was "obscene, lewd, lascivious, and filthy," and the case went to court. Four years later, the U.S. Supreme Court unanimously reversed the finding that the postmaster in Los Angeles was justified in seizing copies of *ONE*. This was the first major legal victory for the gay rights movement in America.

Butch/Femme

HONESTLY, the Mattachine Society never paid a whole lot of attention to women. The group had started off with men, and new members were usually men because the organization spread by word of mouth. Also, the group focused largely on issues that were important for men—police entrapment, for example, wasn't really an issue for the few middle-class lesbians who showed up at the meetings. So what *was* going on with homosexual women after World War II?

Well, it depends on which of those women you're talking about. For working-class lesbians, the 1950s were the heyday of "butches" and "femmes," social roles that had started taking shape during the 1940s. Historians think the roles may have grown out of the phenomenon of "passing" from earlier in the century. But butches didn't try to pass as men—as much as they took on "masculine" characteristics—they identified as women. Butches were the sexual aggressors in any relationship—some even considered themselves "stone" butches, which meant they wouldn't even let their femme girlfriends *touch* them (or so they claimed). These women were so careful to avoid the appearance of being "flipped," or seduced, by their femmes that some kept all their clothes on during sex. Butches weren't supposed to date other butches, though they were often closer friends than they were with their girlfriends. But it was much more complicated than that: sometimes being butch

Frankie, a 1950s butch.

or femme wasn't a permanent identity, and occasionally a woman would switch, depending on her relationship or even how she felt any particular night.

Remember, the 1940s were a relatively liberating time for women who felt more comfortable in a butch role. For one thing, in factory settings, pants were often part of the dress code. But later on, gay bars were some of the only places women were allowed to wear pants. Hard as it is to believe today, it was illegal in many places for women to dress like men, even in the late 1950s. For instance, butch lesbians in New Orleans knew to wear at least three items of women's clothing in order to avoid being arrested as they walked down the street.

Gay bars were the center of working-class lesbian life, and the butch/femme roles were strictly enforced. Doris Lunden remembered about 1950s New Orleans, "If you didn't pick a role—butch or femme—and stick with that, people thought you were mixed up and you didn't know who you were and you were laughed at and called 'ki-ki'—a sort of queer of the gay world." In the late 1960s, one Springfield, Massachusetts, bar even had separate bathrooms for butches and femmes.

On military bases during the 1950s, informers were planted on women's softball teams.

Playing the roles was also a protective measure for lesbians—if someone walked in who didn't look either butch or femme, that woman was often suspected of being an undercover cop who didn't know any better. As Lisa Ben was well aware during her visits to the If Club and other Los Angeles bars, police raids were common, and those arrested often got strip-searched and thrown in jail for a night. Many bars set up warning systems for raids: in the Canyon Club in Los Angeles, both men and women danced upstairs in homosexual pairs. But if a red light suddenly turned on, that meant the police were on their way up, and everyone switched to form boy-girl couples.

Despite the dangers, gay bars were often the only place for lesbians to go. During the 1950s, softball began attracting large numbers of lesbian participants and spectators. But when the games ended, those women couldn't go anywhere to hang out *except* the bars. (Some gay bars even sponsored softball teams.) Alcoholism was a huge problem among working-class lesbians—the combination of the fact that one had to have a drink in her hand in order to stay in the bar, the masculine appeal of "drinking like a man," and the harsh realities of working-class conditions and social persecution were more than many women could bear.

Among queer theorists, there's some debate about what butch/femme roles meant: Some historians believe the roles were more like "default" roles, since at this time, it was hard for lesbians to imagine a relationship that wasn't masculine/feminine. However, Joan Nestle and Judy Grahn have argued that butches weren't copying men, they were copying other lesbians. The role demonstrated another way women could act.

Mother Bilitis

WHATEVER THE REASONS BEHIND "butches" and "femmes," many middle- and upper-class women weren't having any of it. They didn't feel comfortable in the roles, they hated the bars with their depressing alcoholics, and they definitely weren't looking to be involved in anything that regularly resulted in a police raid.

In 1953, the same year of the Mattachine coup, Del Martin and Phyllis Lyon moved to San Francisco together. Not fans of gay bars, they tried to find a different way to meet other lesbians. Eventually, Martin and Lyon joined three other lesbian couples in 1955 to form their own social club that they called the Daughters of Bilitis (DOB). The name was derived from Pierre Louÿs's collection of erotic poems, *Songs of Bilitis*. The pair later stated that they wanted an obscure name that "would sound like any other women's lodge. . . . If anyone asked us, we could always say we belonged to a poetry club."

The Ladder

OCTOBER, 1957

The women quickly realized that they were spending a lot of time complaining about how hard it was for lesbians, and Martin and Lyon suggested making the social club something with a more educational purpose, like the Mattachine Society. The couple devoted themselves to their fledgling organization, answering letters, hosting meetings, paying many of the organization's bills, as well as editing and writing the monthly magazine, *The Ladder*. The magazine was not very political—mostly poetry, fiction, history, and biography—and it upheld many of the homophile beliefs in conformity with mainstream culture. The basic message was, "don't rock the boat, let's try to get them to like us. We're not really different, we just happen to be attracted to women." (Years later, a former DOB member wryly noted: "The magazine was called *The Ladder* because you were supposed to climb up the ladder and into the human race on an OK basis.")

The Daughters of Bilitis focused on the welfare of its own members, providing them a comforting place to go and discuss their problems and make social connections. Like Mattachine, DOB avoided thinking of homosexuals as an oppressed minority—the term "variant" was preferred over "lesbian" in DOB's statement of purpose. In order to become more acceptable to society, the group formally disapproved of anything butch. This annoyed many of the members—Lorraine Hansberry, a famous black playwright, wrote to *The Ladder* in 1957 to remind the organization that "[O]ne is oppressed or discriminated against because one is different, not 'wrong' or 'bad' somehow" (though she, too, supported some conformity measures). Kay Lahusen, an early member of DOB on the East Coast who went by "Kay Tobin" in the 1960s and 1970s, recalled, "As I quickly learned, the purpose of DOB was to get gay people to jack themselves up. If you were a lesbian, you were to put on a skirt and join the human race."

Despite the caution, the Daughters of Bilitis was doing something completely unique and scary for the time, and the group attracted new members—slowly. (A massive revolution this was not.) Barbara Gittings formed an East Coast chapter in 1958, and by 1960 there were five chapters with a total of 110 members (in San Francisco, New York, Chicago, Rhode Island, and Los Angeles—where Lisa Ben had been a member). Mattachine that year could boast only 230 members belonging to chapters in those five locations, along with Detroit, Denver, Philadelphia, and Washington, D.C. This was a terrifying time for gays and lesbians, who were commonly fired from their jobs, arrested by undercover police, or harassed—even physically assaulted—for being different. Very few people were willing to take risks like joining an organization. Lahusen later explained, "Frankly, in the beginning days of the movement, the people who turned up were, by and large, pretty oddball. It's only from the most oddball fringey-type gay people that we have worked our way into the mainstream of the gay minority."

Though the two homophile organizations didn't always get along (mostly, DOB resented the Mattachine's patronizing, sexist attitudes and male-centered agenda, while Mattachine didn't see why DOB had to be a separate organization), they did work together frequently to host joint events. Their shared homophile philosophy of making connections with experts sometimes led to bizarre results: the groups would invite lecturers, and occasionally the "expert" would explain to them how homosexuals were sick and destined for unhappiness if they didn't get themselves cured. Gittings later noted:

It's amazing to people now that we put up with some of the nonsense that was parlayed in these lectures. And yet, we had to go through that because we really needed the recognition that we got from these people who were names in law, the ministry, and the mental health professions. . . . That was important—just their coming and recognizing our existence gave us a boost. . . . People . . . talked about homosexuality being a sickness. . . . We'd sit there and listen and politely applaud and then go for the social hour afterward.

RIGHT: Playwright Lorraine Hansberry. March 1959.

OPPOSITE: *The Ladder: A Lesbian Review.* October 1957.

Dissipation

THE NATIONAL MATTACHINE ORGANIZATION fell apart by the end of the decade. In 1959, the Mattachine Society held its national convention in Denver. The event was a success, and the organization received plenty of press coverage. Unfortunately, two morals officers attended the meeting undercover. After the conference, the police raided the homes of the chapter leaders in Denver, arresting one for violating a local antipornography statute—he ended up leaving Denver soon after. The press reported that the cops seized a mailing list of organization members, and the Denver branch disappeared.

By 1961, the New York Mattachine group had grown the largest. They accused the national organization leaders in California of "fiscal irregularities," prompting Call to dissolve the national structure. Several of the branches folded, but some, like the New York group, continued operating independently.

Maybe the early homophiles weren't as politically effective as they could have been, with a more revolutionary perspective and a clear agenda. But keep in mind that 1950s America was extremely homophobic, and lesbians and gays were terrified. It took a great deal of courage to go to a gay meeting—or a gay bar, for that matter—knowing that you were putting your job, your reputation, and even your safety at risk. But these determined individuals took that step, and in doing so they offered encouragement as well as helpful services to other gays and lesbians—including referrals for discreet doctors to treat sexually transmitted diseases, fair lawyers for entrapment cases or children's custody battles, and understanding mental health workers to help with the psychological strain of a hostile world. But perhaps their most valuable service was letting others (and themselves, really) actually see that they were not alone.

Hearing the Beats

AS THE HOMOPHILES TRIED IN VAIN to transform society from within, a different group of people was transforming society from the outside . . . way outside. On October 7, 1955, writer Allen Ginsberg read his landmark poem *Howl* in a San Francisco gallery. The poem began, "I saw the best minds of my generation destroyed by madness. . . ." and it went on to list a vivid variety of experiences, including several explicitly gay encounters. The poem became an anthem for a generation of rebels, people who didn't fit in to the rigid orthodoxy of 1950s America. Ginsberg and his friends Jack Kerouac and William S. Burroughs were the founding fathers of "the Beats," a countercultural

BELOW: An early photograph of Beat Generation friends Hal Chase, Jack Kerouac, Allen Ginsberg, and William S. Burroughs (left to right) in Morningside Heights, near the Columbia University campus in New York. 1944 or 1945.

movement that, not unlike the Greenwich Village bohemians of fifty years before, celebrated deviation from the norm, often through writing, sex, and drugs. The sexually graphic language of *Howl* became famous—customs officials seized copies of the poem in 1957 (the poem was being printed in London), and when San Francisco's City Lights bookstore published it, the owner was unsuccessfully charged with obscenity.

Ginsberg and Burroughs were confirmed homosexuals, but even predominantly heterosexual Beatniks were open to homosexual experiences. As historian Charles Kaiser pointed out, "In this postwar period, they were the first group of American writers ever to portray homosexuality as hip—a huge step forward for all those who continued to accept society's definition of this orientation as an illness, a crime, or both." Many of the Beats' hangouts in the North Beach section of San Francisco and the Greenwich Village area of New York overlapped with gay hangouts. The Beats' attitude of resistance undoubtedly influenced an evolving gay culture as America entered the radical 1960s.

"What is a lesbian? A lesbian is the rage of all women condensed to the point of explosion."

—RADICALESBIANS, "THE WOMAN IDENTIFIED WOMAN," 1970

4 : BRING IT ON

: 1960–1979

San Francisco, 1965

NANCY MAY JUST KNEW this was going to be a historic night.

Was it because of the klieg lights the police had set up at the entrance of California Hall? Or the photographs they were taking of every person going inside? Or the fact that the police had blocked off every intersection, diverting traffic? They even had helmets and riot gear and motorcycles and paddy wagons parked at the ready.

Nope. Nancy knew tonight was historic because people were still coming in.

About five hundred people had made advance donations in order to attend, and already there were about two hundred people inside California Hall. A lot of people turned away when they saw the commotion, of course, but others drove their limousines right up front and marched straight up to it.

It helped that a lot of the partygoers were in full costume. The police had preprinted arrest cards with numbers on them, and they attached the photographs to the cards for faster processing if things got ugly. True, it was a bit odd to have a Mardi Gras party on New Year's Day, but normally you could dress in drag only on Halloween without the police arresting you. Initially, the police had said they would allow the event, but then—well, all bets were off now with this mess.

The ball was a fund-raiser for the Council on Religion and the Homosexual (CRH), an organization recently formed by sixteen ministers and various gay activists. Ted McIlvenna, a minister-social worker with the Glide Memorial Methodist Church in the poor, rough Tenderloin district of San Francisco, had realized that many of the teen runaways he was trying to help were homosexuals who had been thrown into the streets by their families. The more he learned about how gays and lesbians were treated by society—and particularly by Christian churches—the more concerned he grew. Ted decided to start bringing homosexual activists together with Protestant ministers to discuss what might be done, and after a successful four-day retreat last year, they created CRH. One of the member groups was the Society for Individual Rights (SIR), and Nancy was the chairperson of SIR's political committee.

Nancy wasn't wearing a costume; she was just there to help run the event. Phyllis Lyon and Del Martin were at the front table, keeping track of the donation receipts. Nancy watched as her husband, Bill, took pictures of the police outside. He was so focused, so steadfast.

She was reminded of the first time she laid eyes on Bill—she thought he was the most beautiful person she had ever seen. She knew from the beginning that he was gay, of course, but the attraction was still so strong. . . .

Bill came up to Nancy and whispered in her ear, "Here." He handed her two rolls of film. "I know that nothing's going to happen to you, so take this film and do something with it."

Cops Invade Homosexual Benefit Ball

The police moved in on a homosexual benefit ball sponsored by Protestant ministers last night—and arrested two attorneys who protested.

The affair was conducted by the Council for Religion and the Homosexual, which has been established by Episcopal, Methodist, Lutheran and United Church of Christ leaders to try to integrate homosexuals into the Christian community.

Three police cars were stationed outside the scene, at California Hall, Polk street and Golden Gate avenue, and a police photographer took pictures of arriving homosexuals and their friends, the ministers said.

At about 10 p. m., Inspectors Rudolph Nieto and Richard Castro, from the sex crimes detail, entered the hall, but were met by two attorneys for the council, Evander Smith, 42, with offices at 333 Franklin street, and Herbert Donaldson, 37, of 6 Lloyd street.

They advised the inspectors they had no right to inspect the private party without a search warrant, said the Rev. Ted McIlvenna of the Glide Foundation, one of the sponsoring organizations.

The attorneys were arrested on charges of interfering with police officers in the performance of their duty, and taken to Northern Station.

The Rev. Lewis E. Durham, program director of the foundation, said the Right Rev. James A. Pike, Episcopal Bishop of California, talked over the plans with Police Chief Thomas Cahill last week—but the police later tried to persuade the operators of California Hall to cancel the rental agreement with the council.

Ministers on hand when the police moved in included the Rev. Clarence Colwell, United Church of Christ, the Rev. A. Cecil Williams, a Methodist, director of the foundation's Church and Community section, the Rev. Charles Lewis of the Lutheran, North Beach Mission, and Canon Robert Romey of Grace Cathedral.

The Rev. Mr. Durham said the police action was a surprise because "we thought the whole thing had calmed down."

Nancy couldn't help feeling a little thrill. Bill had been taking pictures for an hour, and the police had been coming in every fifteen minutes to do an "inspection." First it was the fire inspection. Then it was the health inspection. They tried to intimidate the partygoers by walking around the bar and the dance floor, opening up the closets. They would look inside, staring at the chairs stored within, acting as if they had never seen a closet before.

After several of these "inspections," Herbert Donaldson and Evander Smith, lawyers for the CRH, told the police that they couldn't come in again unless they brought the fire chief or a warrant with them. The police simply picked up Herb and Evander by the elbows, legs dangling in the air, and hauled them into a paddy wagon.

Twenty minutes had passed since the lawyers had been arrested. Nancy walked over to the front table. She figured most of the excitement with the police was over. She told Phyllis and Del, "If you guys want to go in and see the show, I'll take over the table here." They gave her a grateful look, and made their way inside.

Nancy was supposed to work the table with another volunteer, but the guy had never arrived. Nancy sighed, picked up some more of the half-filled drinking cups, and walked over to the trash can.

Suddenly a huge man stopped right in front of her. Nancy, mind you, stood five feet two inches high and weighed 110 pounds. The guy was probably six feet four, 215 pounds.

"We're coming in to inspect the premises," he told her.

"No, you're not," she snapped back. "I've just about had it with you people."

The man's face hardened. "Look, lady, we're coming in." He shoved a badge in Nancy's face.

Nancy almost laughed. "That doesn't make any difference to me," she retorted. "You don't have a warrant. You don't belong here. Now get out!"

And he did.

San Francisco Chronicle article "Cops Invade Homosexual Benefit Ball." January 2, 1965.

Whoa, thought Nancy. *That was easy.*

But then he came back—with three uniformed policemen. "Put that woman under arrest," he snarled.

Oh, no, thought Nancy, *The film!* She looked around desperately. "Can I get my coat?" she asked. It was a chilly night, and her blouse was sleeveless.

The big man shook his head. "No. Take her out there."

Meanwhile, Cecil Williams, another minister from Glide Memorial, had seen what was going on.

"Let the poor girl get her coat," he said, grabbing Nancy from behind and pulling her toward the coatroom. "For God's sake, man, it's cold out there."

The policemen didn't have an answer to that. In the coatroom, Nancy whispered hurriedly, "Tell Bill that I'm being arrested." Bill Plath, another of SIR's founders, had hurried over, and she handed him her husband's film. The police had just begun to escort her down the hall toward the front doors when she heard shouting: "You can't take that woman! You can't take that woman! You can't come in here anymore. . . ."

The police grabbed the wild-eyed man as well, and the two were taken out to an empty paddy wagon.

The shouting man was Elliott Leighton, one more lawyer whom Herb and Evander had asked to be on standby that night. Nancy was glad for the companionship, and Elliott was absolutely furious. Nancy was mad, too, and she was surprised to find that she wasn't scared at all.

What the police were doing wasn't right. It just wasn't right.

THE POLICE STRIP-SEARCHED ELLIOTT LEIGHTON at Northern Station, even though bail had already been paid. The next day, the ministers called a press conference to publicly criticize the police department for what had happened, and the newspapers were soon brimming with stories about police harassment. The American Civil Liberties Union (ACLU) was so angered by the way the event was handled by the police, the organization decided to provide the lawyers' and Nancy's defense in court. In any case, they didn't have to lift a finger—the judge instructed the jury to return a not-guilty verdict before the defense even got to argue, saying, "It's useless to waste everybody's time following this to its finale." Inspired by the event, CRH began a study of local law enforcement practices, and soon after they helped form Citizens Alert, a twenty-four-hour hotline for people to report police brutality.

The episode marked a shift in attitude for San Franciscan gays and lesbians. Times were changing, and they just weren't going to put up with harassment anymore.

RIGHT: Shirley
MacLaine (left) as
Martha Dobie and
Audrey Hepburn as
Karen Wright in the
film *The Children's
Hour.* 1961.

OPPOSITE: "Randy
Wicker" fields
questions from
viewers during a
phone-in segment of
The Les Crane Show,
on WABC-TV,
New York. January
31, 1964.

Look, Honey, Homosexuals!

THE EARLY 1960s saw a gradual increase in the amount of public discussion about homosexuality by the heterosexual mainstream—much to the benefit of gays and lesbians across the country. Lesbian pulp novels, though written primarily to titillate straight men, were collected and treasured by many women just discovering and attempting to understand their homosexuality. In 1961, Hollywood's Production Code was finally revised to allow showing homosexuality in movies—that is, with "care, discretion, and restraint." That year, big-name actresses Audrey Hepburn and Shirley MacLaine starred in a silver screen version of Lillian Hellman's *The Children's Hour,* and one year later, in *Advise & Consent,* the character played by Don Murray was blackmailed for his homosexual past. Although both movies were a bit morbid, they did include somewhat sympathetic views of homosexuality. Not only that, but newspapers and magazines such as *The New York Times, Newsweek, Life, Time, Look,* and *Harpers* began running articles on the underground homosexual culture found in large cities. Though some of these articles weren't exactly positive, they did offer many gays and lesbians all over the country information about where and how to find others like themselves.

The PR Machine

MANY OF THOSE ARTICLES were arranged by a young guy from New Jersey who went by the name "Randy Wicker" (his real name was Charles Hayden). When Wicker was a college student, he spent the summer of 1958 helping out the Mattachine Society in New York. To help publicize one of the group's lectures, Wicker went to different shops around New York to put up posters—thanks to his efforts, the number of attendees tripled to three hundred. But when Wicker went back to school in the fall, no one else would risk distributing the posters, and participation fell once again. In his last two years of college in Texas, Wicker became very active in the civil rights movement, so when he moved back to New York after graduation in 1961, he was psyched to put his energy into gay organizing. Wicker started by going to gay bars around the city to pass out information about the Mattachine Society—and he was surprised to find that many of the men there were annoyed by what he was doing. Many gay New Yorkers didn't want to change the way the general public thought about homosexuals because they figured they were living safely under the radar as long as they didn't act effeminate or flamboyant in public. Even the Mattachine leaders weren't too thrilled with Wicker's sense of initiative—he proposed plans for greater press coverage of the organization, but the leadership was scared that media attention without "expert" backing such as sympathetic psychiatrists would only cause a negative reaction.

That wasn't good enough for Wicker. He could see that progress wasn't possible without visibility. Wicker founded the Homosexual League of New York in 1962. This new organization had only one member—guess who? Wicker, presenting himself as a "representative" of the league, managed to convince a local radio station to broadcast a show in which seven gay men spoke about their lives, and then he sent out press releases. When a conservative columnist took the bait and criticized the station for hosting the show, Wicker got lots more attention for it; even *Newsweek* and *The New York Times* ran sympathetic articles about the broadcast.

Wicker was on a roll. Each new article made it easier for him to interest more and more news sources in reporting stories about

the gay world. He took reporters on tours of the Greenwich Village gay scene, provided information on legal concerns, was interviewed on television, and managed to get invitations to speak at colleges and various other institutions. His new visibility even got him a regular column in Mattachine's own newsletter, where he promoted his aggressive ideas.

Don't Mess with Astronomers

EANWHILE, IN WASHINGTON, D.C., things were heating up. Dr. Franklin Kameny, an astronomer with a Harvard Ph.D., had been fired from his job at the U.S. Army map service back in 1957 because of his homosexuality—and barred from any future federal employment. (He had been arrested at a popular D.C. cruising spot, though the charges were quickly dropped.) Kameny was outraged at the unfairness of the situation. He tried everything he could think of to appeal, and his record of homosexuality was keeping him from getting a new job. By 1961, he could see that he wasn't getting anywhere; his cause needed the support of an organization. So, he decided to start one up: he cofounded the Mattachine Society of Washington, D.C., and was elected its first president.

Kameny brought new life to the homophile movement. He was articulate, bold, and unim-

TOP: Among Franklin Kameny's many contributions to gay rights was helping create the Gay and Lesbian Alliance of Washington, D.C., an organization that continues to lobby government and press for equal rights. 1971.

BOTTOM: ECHO Convention. 1965.

pressed by the authority of so-called experts, and he had a very clear vision of what needed to be done. (And he was smart—he had started college when he was only fifteen.) With his arrest record hindering his job prospects, he also had little to lose.

Kameny's first priority was his personal "war" with the federal government over the ban of homosexuals from civil employment. In 1962, Washington Mattachine wrote letters to every single major government leader (including those in Congress, the Supreme Court, the Cabinet, and the White House) to schedule appointments to discuss the issue. And for the next year, the organization kept at it, trying to arrange meetings, and then attempting to achieve meaningful dialogue with officials who finally caved. Kameny eventually got the D.C. branch of the American Civil Liberties Union involved in the fight. In turn, the D.C. branch pressured the national organization to reconsider its position on homosexuality; in 1957, the national ACLU had declared its support of sodomy statutes as well as the ban of gays and lesbians from government jobs. But by 1964, the national organization pulled a complete 180° on its position, thereby encouraging its branches to take on gay rights cases. Kameny made some enemies, too—in 1963, Representative John Dowdy of Texas tried to pass a bill revoking Washington Mattachine's permit to raise money. Kameny argued Mattachine's case in Congressional hearings, and with favorable press and the ACLU's help, he managed to get the bill killed in the Senate. He was just getting started.

I'm Sick? Prove It

KAMENY BELIEVED IT WAS IMPORTANT for homophile organizations to say to the world, "We're *not* sick." His own scientific credentials gave him the insight and authority to reject the shoddy academic work that was being passed off as "evidence" for a psychiatric disorder. In 1964, he delivered a speech to the New York Mattachine group stating that the "entire homophile movement is going to stand or fall upon the question of whether homosexuality is a sickness, and upon our taking a firm stand on it." Though the old guard of the Mattachine wasn't too happy to hear this, the members were thrilled—within a year, the leadership had been replaced by Kameny-style activists. In 1965, the Washington Mattachine formally approved an antisickness resolution, and the New York group soon followed suit. Homophile organizations along the East Coast had joined in an annual conference called East Coast Homophile Organizations (ECHO) to help coordinate their efforts. In 1965, ECHO's new leaders pushed a radical agenda that included public picketing. In some ways, the changes of 1965 were the Mattachine leadership coup of 1953 in reverse: the old, "let's-listen-to-experts" homophile leaders were leaving the organization while more militant activists were taking over.

Except in the Daughters of Bilitis, that is. Barbara Gittings became the editor of *The Ladder* in 1962, just after she had heard Randy Wicker give a speech a couple months before. She loved what he had said, and then in 1963, she met Franklin Kameny at an ECHO conference. Gittings and Kameny became friends, and soon Gittings was getting frustrated with the DOB's dependence on so-called authorities who weren't doing anything to help homosexuals. She made *The Ladder* more radical, adding the word "lesbian" to the cover and including articles that supported her aggressive views toward direct political action. The leadership in New York and San Francisco weren't amused. After ECHO decided to organize political protests in 1965, DOB pulled out of the organization— and Gittings and other radicals left DOB to work independently. While the Mattachine groups in New York and D.C. grew because of their new energy (the members in New York's group more than doubled to 445 in a year), New York's DOB numbers stayed wee—in fact, in the summer of 1965, they probably had less than fifty members.

The Homosexual Capital

MEANWHILE, ON THE WEST COAST, where the homophile movement had begun, progress was afoot. In 1959, San Francisco mayoral candidate Russell Wolden figured he could score votes by warning San Franciscans that their city was becoming the capital of homosexuality in the United States. He was wrong—about scoring votes, that is. Newspapers started attacking him for "stigmatizing" the city, and Wolden ultimately lost the race. Because of Wolden's political mistake, the city's gay and lesbian organizations got positive exposure in the press, and homosexuals all over the country were reading in the papers that San Francisco was the place to be.

Admittedly, Wolden was on to something. A lot of gay and lesbian veterans had stayed in San Francisco after the Second World War, and the homosexual population *did* grow steadily—one city newspaper in 1949 ran the front-page headline, "HOMOS INVADE S.F." This population growth was helped by the fact that in 1951 California's Supreme Court had ordered the reinstatement of the liquor license of San Francisco's Black Cat gay bar (also a favorite hangout of the Beats)—gay men and lesbians in California were guaranteed their right to assemble in a public establishment. (However, this didn't stop police from harassing them on other "misconduct" charges. In 1955, the state legislature passed a law outlawing "resorts for . . . sexual perverts" in an attempt to justify the ongoing raids of gay bars.)

Soon after the mayoral election, the situation for homosexuals in San Francisco worsened dramatically. The owner of a gay bar reported to the district attorney's office that he had been forced

"HOMOS INVADE S.F.," from an issue of the San Francisco tabloid *The Truth*. July 11, 1949.

to give the police bribes for more than two years in order to stay open, and several other bars joined the complaint. The media went to town on the "gayola" corruption investigation, and the police became angry. The police chief announced that he had reorganized his force for "an attack on San Francisco's homosexual problem" and stepped up harassment—soon the police were clocking forty to sixty misdemeanor charges against women and men at the bars per week. In August 1961, eighty-nine men and fourteen women were arrested in a bar raid at the Tay-Bush Inn, the biggest such raid in the city's history.

Vote for the Queen

IN 1961, JOSÉ SARRIA was "the best known and loved gay man in San Francisco," as historian John D'Emilio described him. A drag performer at the Black Cat bar, Sarria performed comedic operas every Sunday afternoon—shows that he rewrote to reflect gay men's concerns, like avoiding the police while cruising for sex. At the end of each performance, he would make his audience stand, put their arms around one another, and sing "God Save Us Nelly Queens." One man later remembered,

"You must realize that the vice squad was there. . . . They used to come in and stand around and just generally intimidate people and make them feel that they were less than human." But, he said, "To be able to stand up and sing, 'God Save Us Nelly Queens'—we were really not saying 'God Save Us Nelly Queens.' We were saying 'We have our rights too.'"

The city of San Francisco is run by a board of supervisors, as well as the mayor. And in 1961, just when the police crackdown was at its worst, Sarria decided to run for city supervisor. He got only six thousand votes in the end, but he succeeded in shaking up the homosexual population, forcing them to think about themselves as having political potential.

Politics + Fun = Success

IN 1961, the same year that Randy Wicker began taking Mattachine materials to New York's gay bars, the League for Civil Education (a brand-new homophile group in San Francisco) started publishing *LCE News* and passing it out at the city's gay bars (places homophile groups traditionally tried to avoid). The combination of the social (bars) and the political (headlines like "WE MUST FIGHT NOW") proved to be an immediate success in San Francisco—within a year, LCE was printing seven thousand copies an issue, more copies than national magazines like *ONE*, *The Ladder*, and the *Mattachine Review* combined. At the same time, a group of San Francisco gay bars formed the Tavern Guild to provide coordinated legal defense against arrests and harassment of gay establishments. Then in 1964, Bill and Nancy May, Bill Plath, and other friends founded the Society for Individual Rights (SIR) to focus on building a community of homosexuals in San Francisco; SIR was an inclusive organization that was open to anything its members wanted to do. With almost a thousand members within two years, SIR became the largest homophile organization in the country. The group started various activities, anything from bowling to meditation sessions to art classes. SIR eventually opened a thrift shop to fund these activities, and in 1966 the group set up the first gay community center in the country.

It was in this political context that the police harassment at CRH's 1965 New Year's Day Ball made headlines. The incident proved that homosexuals on the West Coast were entering a new era of resistance and on a much larger scale. Meanwhile, the proconformity homophile organizations such as Mattachine and DOB didn't take a strong public stand, and they became increasingly obsolete as their members gravitated to more aggressive organizations.

Let's Take This Outside

BACK ON THE EAST COAST, the newly radicalized homophile groups began imitating the direct-action protests that were made famous by the civil rights movement of black Americans. Beginning in 1965, activists at ECHO organized picket-line protests of government discrimination in the White House, the State Department, and the Pentagon. They also planned an Annual Reminder picketing at Independence Hall in Philadelphia on July Fourth to remind the general public that homosexuals didn't have the same freedoms as other Americans. Truthfully, there were usually only about thirty or forty people marching at any one protest, where the men dressed in suits and the women wore skirts and heels. But it was still an electrifying experience for most participants. Barbara Gittings later recalled, "It was thrilling. You knew you were doing something momentous. People would stare at you. They had never seen self-declared homosexuals parading with signs."

LEFT: A group of "homosexual American citizens" picket in Washington, D.C., on Armed Forces Day. May 21, 1965.

OPPOSITE: Herb Donaldson at the time of his arrest at the CRH's New Year's Day Ball. 1965.

Shirley Willer, a DOB leader in New York, remembered, "We had to do the public protests because people never got the chance to see what a gay person looked like. Everybody was in the closet! Until they saw people who said publicly that they were gay, they couldn't know that we looked like every other human being—that we had faces, ears, and noses, that we dressed the same and had the same kinds of jobs." Unfortunately, the protests never generated much media attention—but with every picketing, the homophile activists became more and more energized.

In New York, Mattachine president Dick Leitsch and two other Mattachine members, Craig Rodwell and John Timmons, held a "sip-in" in 1966 to protest the State Liquor Authority's policy of closing down bars that served homosexuals. The three men took a group of reporters with them to various Village bars, and gave each bartender a statement declaring their homosexuality. The first two bars gave them drinks anyway, but when the third finally refused, the New York Mattachine filed a complaint with the State Liquor Authority. The case went to court, and in 1967 an appellate court ruled that serving a homosexual was not reason enough to revoke a liquor license.

Spreading the Word

HOMOPHILE ORGANIZATIONS FROM ALL OVER THE COUNTRY came together during the summer of 1966 to form a national organization that would eventually settle on the name NACHO, the North American Conference of Homophile Organizations. This new group took on legal cases, produced studies on homosexuality and the law, and coordinated protests all over the country. In 1968, NACHO adopted Kameny's suggestion of "Gay Is Good" as a slogan for the homophile movement (taking inspiration from the civil rights movement's "Black Is Beautiful"). NACHO's growing membership reflected the fact that homophile groups were popping up all over, including in Kansas City, Missouri; Seattle, Washington; Syracuse, New York; Houston, Texas; Richmond, Virginia; and Cincinnati and Columbus, Ohio. In 1966, Mattachine had fifteen branches—by the spring of 1969, there were fifty.

Left Behind

THINGS WERE FINALLY MOVING ALONG within the homophile movement—and yet, when you put it in perspective, its gains were far behind those of other civil rights movements. Despite growing numbers, gay organizations did not constitute a mass movement—in fact, a mid-1960s study showed that only 2 percent of American homosexuals were even aware that homophile organizations existed. Meanwhile, black Americans were out in the streets demonstrating for their rights, and they were winning a series of sweeping federal acts prohibiting racial discrimination. The women's liberation movement was growing in strength as thousands of women flocked to the newly formed National Organization of Women (NOW). The group soon began a drive to revive a proposed Equal Rights Amendment (ERA) to the U.S. Constitution that would explicitly eliminate gender discrimination. College students, too, were gathering en masse, protesting the Vietnam War and arguing for something they called "participatory democracy," a philosophy that sought to expand the people's role in making public decisions.

Homosexuals across America needed a wake-up call if they were ever going to tap into the revolutionary currents all around them.

A Star Is Dead

ON SUNDAY, JUNE 22, 1969, Judy Garland, the actress who played Dorothy in *The Wizard of Oz*, died from an overdose of drugs at the age of forty-seven. Garland had been a favorite concert singer among gay men for decades—she was often over-the-top in her performances. With emotions ranging from heartbreaking vulnerability to giddy happiness, she became *the* quintessential gay icon. Gays would crowd her concerts, and they commonly used the phrase "friend of Dorothy" to euphemistically identify other homosexual men.

An estimated twenty thousand people waited for hours to pay their respects to Garland during two days in the humid Manhattan summer heat outside the funeral home. For many gay people, those were days of grief.

Judy Garland leans over the footlights to greet some of her enthusiastic fans during her concert at Carnegie Hall. April 23, 1961.

Stonewall

BUT GRIEF QUICKLY TURNED TO RAGE that Friday night, June 27, in a New York City gay bar. The Stonewall Inn on Christopher Street was a dingy bar with its front window painted black that served watered-down drinks in unwashed glasses. The customers were almost all men, often including a few drag queens, with the occasional butch lesbian. Technically, the place was listed as a private "bottle club" in order to get around the need for a liquor license, which meant that the owners weren't supposed to *sell* the drinks—which of course they did anyway. Customers had to sign their names in a book by the entrance, just in case it would be needed in court for proof that they were members of the club ("Judy Garland," "Donald Duck," and "Elizabeth Taylor" were frequent visitors). The Mafia owners paid about $2,000 a week in bribes to the police to stay open,

The Stonewall Inn after the riots, Greenwich Village, New York.

but even so, the bar was raided about once a month. The bar had warning lights that flashed when the police were on their way in so that customers could stop dancing and touching, and so that the bartenders had time to jump the bar and pretend to be customers (to better their chances of not getting arrested). The weekly bribes usually bought the bar a heads-up tip from the police that they were on their way—but on June 27, the tip didn't come.

That night, the warning lights flashed, and eight detectives barged in. The raid started off with the usual insults and rough handling. The police arrested some customers, but let most of them go. There was a crowd outside the bar that night, and when departing drag queens left, they struck poses for the cheering onlookers. When police paddy wagons pulled up to take away the arrested customers, the crowd's mood suddenly shifted. Enough was enough. As the police came out of the bar, the bystanders began yelling. Then they started throwing bottles and coins.

The police were stunned—this had never happened at a gay bar raid. Homosexuals didn't fight back. Someone threw a garbage can through the bar's front window, and the police got scared. They retreated back into the bar. Craig Rodwell was in the crowd, and he ran to a pay phone to call the major New York newspapers to get reporters sent to Christopher Street. Someone squirted lighter fluid into the bar through the broken window and began throwing in lit matches. The police tried to come outside, but the crowd wouldn't let up—one police officer grabbed a hostage and pulled him in. They beat the man and arrested him for assault. (The hostage turned out to be a heterosexual folk singer, Dave Van Ronk.) Then the police tried to spray the crowd with a fire hose from inside the bar, but the crowd just laughed and roared louder. Finally, a riot control unit arrived and freed the trapped policemen—but the crowd didn't back down. A wild group of drag queens formed a high-kicking chorus line and sang:

We are the Stonewall girls
We wear our hair in curls
We wear no underwear
We show our pubic hair
We wear our dungarees
Above our nelly knees!

The street was in chaos: police beating people, people throwing concrete blocks and garbage at police cars. Among the casualties of that night were two fingers that a teenager lost when his hand was slammed in a car door, and there were puddles of blood in the streets where cops had singled out young "feminine boys" for a beating. But a total of only thirteen people were arrested that night, seven of whom were Stonewall employees.

All throughout the next day, people came by to check out the scene of the trashed bar. Someone had scrawled "Support Gay Power" and "Legalize Gay Bars" on the entrance, and a crowd began to build. That night, the riot control unit returned to confront the thousands of people milling about—soon the street erupted into chaos again, with police randomly beating civilians, and people striking back by throwing bottles and garbage. Passing cars were swallowed by the crowd and rocked, terrorizing the passengers. The chaos lasted until four o'clock in the morning, when the last of the police left.

Momentum

NOT EVERYONE UNDERSTOOD THE MEANING of these events right away—many of the wealthier gays who had spent the weekend on Fire Island, a popular gay weekend destination outside New York City, were just glad the tacky bar was gone. Even a rabble-rouser like Randy Wicker wasn't happy about what happened. As he put it, "Screaming queens forming chorus lines and kicking went against everything that I wanted people to think about homosexuals . . . that we were a bunch of drag queens in the Village acting disorderly and tacky and cheap." (Does that sentiment seem familiar? Remember that "queers" distanced themselves from "fairies" earlier in the century, the Daughters of Bilitis formally disapproved of butches, and the Veterans Benevolent Association began excluding flamboyant men in its later years.) Soon a poster appeared alongside the militant messages on the Stonewall Inn's façade:

JOIN THE SISTERS & BROTHERS OF THE **GAY LIBERATION FRONT**

Gay Liberation Front poster, New York. 1970.

WE HOMOSEXUALS PLEAD WITH OUR PEOPLE TO PLEASE HELP MAINTAIN PEACEFUL AND QUIET CONDUCT ON THE STREETS OF THE VILLAGE—MATTACHINE

But whether the homophiles liked it or not, the Stonewall Rebellion was fast becoming a symbol for the entire gay rights movement—or maybe it's more correct to say that in some ways it was creating a new gay rights movement. Allen Ginsberg went to visit the scene of the riot the next day and told a *Village Voice* reporter, "It's about time we did something to assert ourselves." On Sunday, June 29, he went into the reopened bar and declared that the other customers were "beautiful—they've lost that wounded look that fags all had ten years ago."

Gay Power

THE LATE '60s had been one of the most violent, revolutionary periods in modern American history, with several social and political movements converging into what was broadly called the New Left movement. Student demonstrators, Black Power militants, feminist radicals, and anti-Vietnam war activists formed a network of revolt that gave the older generation chills. A group of domestic terrorists known as "Weathermen" or "Weather Underground Organization" organized riots and bombed various (nonhuman) targets across the country to protest the Vietnam War. Long hair, bell-bottom jeans, and a philosophy of free love were the new uniform for activists. Add in a potent mix of LSD and a variety of other drugs, and you have a countercultural mass movement intent on overthrowing the "establishment." It was sex, drugs, and rock 'n' roll—but with an increasingly violent aspect.

New York Mattachine's Dick Leitsch could see the writing on the wall: Stonewall was becoming a call to arms for fringe reactionaries, and he worried that all this unrest would take away the few victories homosexuals had won over the years. He started up a Mattachine Action Committee to try to appease the new radicals who were calling for more action—but he wanted to keep control of them. The committee called a public meeting to discuss the riots and what could be done to take advantage of the new revolutionary spirit. Wearing his brown suit, Leitsch took the microphone and explained the Mattachine approach of education, not violence.

But his audience was in no mood to hear about appeasing the establishment. People began to shout in protest. One attendee, Jim Fouratt, was a young experimental actor with long blond hair who had been involved in various countercultural political movements. He stood up and interrupted the meeting, yelling, "We have got to radicalize. . . . And if it takes riots or even guns to show them what we are, well, that's the only language that the pigs understand!" He then invited everyone to go with him to "Alternate University," a loft space nearby that was used by a variety of radicals, to start up a new organization. And so the Gay Liberation Front (GLF) was born.

GLF's rallying call for "Gay Power" drew an energetic membership together. The group immediately started passing out leaflets reading, "DO YOU THINK HOMOSEXUALS ARE REVOLTING?" Then below, "YOU BET YOUR SWEET ASS WE ARE." The group planned a demonstration in which three to four hundred gays marched to the Stonewall Inn one month after the now-famous "rebellion." This group was clearly nothing like the Mattachine, and it began attracting homosexual activists who had kept their homosexuality secret while working in other radical movements. GLF spent a lot of time discussing the gay rights movement in the context of all the other minority movements

Gay Liberation Front sticker. 1970.

at the time, repeatedly explaining that the only way homosexuals could effect real change was if all New Left movements supported one another in their attempts to transform society.

In August 1969, New Left radicals attending the national homophile conference in Kansas City passed resolutions denouncing the Vietnam War and supporting "the black, the feminist, the Spanish-American, the Indian, the Hippie, the Young, the Student, and other victims of oppression and prejudice." In November, GLF went to a gathering of homophile groups on the East Coast and essentially took over. The members voted in resolutions supporting groups such as the Black Panthers and striking West Coast grape pickers, and they endorsed Craig Rodwell's plan for a Stonewall commemorative march. The old guard didn't know what hit them—argumentative, long-haired radicals were destroying their homophile conventions. As Fouratt later admitted, "We wanted to *end* the homophile movement. We wanted them to join *us* in making a gay revolution." Homosexuals were no longer going to try to convince heterosexual society to accept them, they were going to change society itself—or so they believed.

Out of Focus

GAY LIBERATION FRONT participated in a variety of protests during the coming months, not all of them related to gay issues. But the group did make gay visibility a focus—its newsletter was called *Come Out!* The group wanted to offer gays and lesbians an alternative to New York's Mafia-run bars, so it organized dances at the Alternate U. loft space. New York's GLF also sparked the creation of other radical groups in cities across the country, including Philadelphia, Tallahassee, Chicago, Austin, Los Angeles, and San Francisco. By 1973, there would be more than eight hundred groups.

The Los Angeles GLF's first public action targeted a greasy late-night restaurant in West Hollywood called Barney's Beanery. The restaurant had long ago posted a sign above the counter that stated (incorrect spelling included), "Fagots Stay Out." The sign suggested an obvious comparison to "No Colored" lunch counters in the South that were protested during the civil rights movement. In January 1970, a small group of Los Angeles Gay Liberation Front members (led by Rev. Troy Perry, founder of the gay- and lesbian-oriented Metropolitan Community Church) began to protest outside the Beanery. Within weeks, the number of protesters had swelled to a noisy one hundred and fifty. Protesters would go into the restaurant and order a coffee or just one beer—and then stay for hours. After nearly three months of demonstrations that exhausted even the police, the protest ended when Barney's Beanery, without any fanfare, took down its sign at last.

Unfortunately, New York's GLF never lived up to its goals. The meetings were often chaotic, since there were no rules or guidelines—basically, whoever could be the loudest ended up in control. There was a lot of talk about revolution, but little action. GLF founder Martha Shelley later remembered, "We were young and idealistic. . . . The problem was, we had all these platforms, but we never could figure out how to get from here to there." It didn't help that many of the radical groups that they wanted to support didn't support them back; black militant leader Eldridge Cleaver wrote, "Homosexuality is a sickness, just as are baby-rape or wanting to be head of General Motors." Plus, despite GLF's talk about equality, women found the same sexism in the organization they always found—writer Rita Mae Brown and several other women left the group, explaining, "We are no longer willing . . . to be the token women in the Gay Liberation Front."

Within a year, the group had talked itself into oblivion. But even still, GLF marked an important turning point in the consciousness of gay activism.

Back in Business

IN DECEMBER 1969, a group of New York activists who were frustrated by GLF started the Gay Activists Alliance (GAA), an organization that was "completely and solely dedicated" to homosexual rights—and actually had rules and procedures. This new group's goal was not to topple the establishment, but to secure gay rights by using confrontational, militant tactics that went beyond the methods of the homophile radicals of the late '60s.

The most successful method this group developed was the media "zap." GAA cofounder Marty Robinson believed the best way to get support was to really turn the heat up on supposedly "liberal" politicians who *should* have been out there standing up for gay rights. So they approached politicians on the streets, at Democratic clubs, in television studios, or from crowds at public speeches and confronted them directly about their support for gay rights. These scenes often ended up with an activist screaming "ANSWER THE HOMOSEXUAL!" within inches of his target's face. The protests would usually involve a certain amount of theater to get media attention—mock weddings, dressing up as ducks, or taking coffee and doughnuts to magazine staff offices.

TOP: Marty Robinson, leader of the Gay Activists Alliance, "zapping" Nelson A. Rockefeller, the governor of New York, at a Democrats for Rockefeller reception. New York, September 24, 1970.

BOTTOM: Christopher Street Gay Liberation Day march. June 1970.

OPPOSITE: The Firehouse, home of the Gay Activists Alliance. The eleventh letter of the Greek alphabet, lambda, incorporated in the banner, became the best-known symbol of gay rights in the 1970s.

The strategy was remarkably effective. In 1970, GAA began zapping New York Mayor John V. Lindsay, and less than two years later, he endorsed municipal legislation that barred discrimination of homosexuals at work. The group also cornered City Councilwoman Carol Greitzer into cosponsoring the gay rights bill (though it wouldn't pass until 1986).

But the most important effect of these zaps was exposure. GAA's membership exploded, and before long, the group was coordinating up to twenty protests at a time. Two hundred members of GAA led New York City's first pride parade in 1970, called the "Christopher Street Liberation Day Parade," to commemorate the Stonewall riots. These marchers were joined by anywhere from five to twenty thousand other participants, depending on whom you ask, and there were also parades held in Los Angeles and Chicago. GAA became so large that it soon needed a headquarters, and the group settled on an abandoned firehouse in the SoHo area of downtown New York. The 10,000-square-foot space, soon known to every gay New Yorker as the Firehouse, became home to huge dances starting in 1971. These fund-raising dances were unlike anything homosexuals had ever seen in New York—a giant room filled with shirtless men, dancing to blaring music under flashing lights. Activist Ethan Geto remembered, "This was before SoHo was SoHo. This was when SoHo was totally an industrial district. And it was gloomy and dark and foreboding. And in this one place, in the middle of this block on Saturday night, all of a sudden you hear this thumping disco music!" In a few years, this winning concept would be transformed into the huge, glamorous discotheques that dominated New York gay nightlife in the late '70s.

GAA adopted the eleventh letter of the Greek letter, lambda, as its logo. The official reason was something about it symbolizing a "complete exchange of energy"—but really, the designer had picked it because he thought it looked cool. Soon the lambda symbol was all over T-shirts, buttons, signs, and anything the organization printed. It would become the best-known gay rights symbol of the 1970s.

Parents Get Called In

JEANNE MANFORD CLAIMED to be a shy person, someone who never belonged to organizations. Her son Morty, on the other hand, was definitely not shy; he was very active in GAA zaps all over New York City. When Morty was beaten up at one of the protests in April 1972, Jeanne knew she "wasn't going to let anybody walk over Morty." She wrote a letter to the *New York Post* complaining about how the police didn't intervene to protect her son. One thing led to another, and soon this elementary schoolteacher was appearing on television shows as a real-life "gay parent" in Boston, Detroit, New Orleans, and Toronto, among other cities. Then, in 1972, Jeanne marched with Morty in the third annual Christopher Street Liberation Day Parade, carrying a poster that read: "Parents of Gays: Unite in Support of Our Children." Jeanne later remembered, "As we walked along, people on the sidewalks screamed! They yelled! They ran over and kissed me, and asked, 'Will you talk to my mother?'" And so PFLAG (Parents, Families, and Friends of Lesbians and Gays) was born. Chapters began popping up all over the country, ready to give support to parents coming to terms with their children's orientation and actively supporting the gay rights movement. Franklin Kameny's mother joined, too. He remembered, "My mother used to march for me in the Gay Pride March. And they always used to put her in a limousine or sometimes they would have a truck. She marched in

style, and got all the applause." Today, PFLAG comprises more than five hundred chapters worldwide, with more than 200,000 members and supporters working hard toward greater equality for gays and lesbians.

Left Out

TRUTH BE TOLD, women were not a huge part of GAA—even less than they had been in GLF, actually, as the Firehouse dances made clear. Some radical lesbians did start their own small groups, but many more lesbians had become more involved with the women's movement than anything to do with their homosexuality. Unfortunately, many straight women in the women's movement were worried about the age-old accusation "feminists are all lesbians," and they wanted the lesbians out. Betty Friedan, author of the groundbreaking *The Feminine Mystique* and founder of the National Organization of Women (NOW), was one of the movement's most visible leaders. Friedan described lesbians as a "lavender menace" that she believed was threatening the movement.

TOP: Jeanne Manford marched with her son, Morty Manford, in New York City's Christopher Street Liberation Day Parade. 1972.

LEFT: Betty Friedan, president of the National Organization of Women (NOW), holds a Women Power button (left) and an Equality for Women button at a meeting during the organization's fourth annual convention. Chicago, March 21, 1970.

OPPOSITE: Demonstrators carrying signs and banners during the second Gay Pride Parade in New York City. June 27, 1971.

But in May 1970, at the Congress to Unite Women in New York, lesbians took center stage—literally. A group of seventeen women wearing T-shirts declaring themselves the "Lavender Menace" took control of the stage (and therefore the conference) to discuss the problems lesbians were having in the women's movement. The stunt proved to be a watershed success: the congress passed a group of resolutions in support of lesbians, including "whenever the label lesbian is used against the movement collectively or against women individually, it is to be affirmed, not denied." NOW adopted similar positions in the fall of 1971—but to be honest, lesbians weren't totally in the clear: two years later, Friedan would tell *The New York Times* that the CIA was sending agents posing as lesbians to her organization in order to hinder progress. Even still, the Lavender Menace action had given birth to a new movement within feminism: "lesbian-feminists."

Lesbians & Feminists Merge

AFTER THE CONGRESS TO UNITE WOMEN, the Lavender Menaces formed Radicalesbians, one of many new radical groups that promoted the concept of "lesbian-feminism." Feminists argued that men oppressed women and made them second-class citizens, and lesbian-feminists went a step further by insisting that true feminists should free their lives of the influence of men—even in bed. Instead, lesbian-feminists would be "women-identified-women" who put women first in everything. Though some of these new lesbian-feminists were only "political lesbians" (they didn't actually have sex with women), many did choose to pursue homosexual relationships for credibility, even if they had earlier considered themselves straight. Becoming homosexual to them was a *political* choice, not a natural, biological one (as other homosexuals were arguing). Sounding a bit like the prehomosexuality idea of sodomy, claims by activists like Rita Mae Brown were that *any* woman could become a sexual lesbian. Though as historian Lillian Faderman pointed out, lesbianism wasn't that big a stretch for many of the activists: "For many young women who were hippies, lesbianism seemed like just one more exciting adventure, conceivable especially because hippies generally seemed to give at least lip service to the idea that if you grooved on someone, gender was not a major consideration."

These two women, photographed in 1972, exemplify the androgynously butch appearance of lesbian-feminists during the 1970s.

The new lesbian-feminist rejected both the upper/middle-class lesbian identity of a sensible, skirt-wearing woman as well as the butch/femme roles of the working-class bars (the three groups would continue to operate separately). Instead, lesbian-feminists soon developed a new "character" for themselves with an androgynous, slightly butch appearance that often included short hair, unshaved armpits and legs, jeans, natural-fiber shirts, and boots. Lesbian-feminists talked about building a utopian Lesbian Nation by creating woman-centered communities free of "male" values like authority and dominance. Some lesbian-feminists who were called separatists even believed that it was important to remove *all* men from their personal and political lives and that women should build up a self-sufficient society. Lesbian-feminist groups started food co-ops, credit unions, and health clinics. Many insisted on spelling woman as "womyn," "wimmin," or "womben" to eliminate even the word "man," just as history became "herstory" and hurricane became "hisicane." They also embraced the word "dyke" as a term for themselves in order to take away the word's power as an insult. There was a big focus on ancient societies led by women, as well as renewed interest in witchcraft and historical figures who were accused of being witches—in the lesbian-feminist view, these women were persecuted because their strength and independence challenged male power.

"Women's Music" was probably the strongest connection among lesbian-feminists, with hugely successful women's festivals drawing thousands all across the country. Olivia Records, started in 1973, was the leading women's music record company, and it managed to sell out huge national tours for its recording artists, notably Cris Williamson, Margie Adam, and Holly Near. Women's music became known for its political, angry, and affirmative lyrics about women's/lesbians' value. The festivals where women's music was performed also included political workshops on lesbian topics, and they were *extremely* politically correct—they often offered vegetarian options, day care, interpreters for the deaf, a sliding scale of admission for poor, and "chemical-free" areas for people who weren't comfortable with the drug use often found at festivals. There was even a big debate about whether women could bring their male children. (Their presence was upsetting to some separatists who wanted to live their lives entirely separate from men, even young boys.) Perhaps the most successful festival was the Michigan Womyn's Music Festival, first staged in 1976, which still attracts thousands of women every August from all over the world.

Yet by the end of the 1970s most lesbian-feminist groups had crashed and burned, broken up over interpersonal conflicts and the sheer exhaustion of having to be politically correct in everything. But lesbian-feminists were similar to GLF; their forceful positions set an example for *all* lesbians to feel pride and demand more from the world. Also, perhaps because lesbian separatist groups were so extreme in demanding complete separation, mainstream society was more willing to consider the appeals of traditional gay and lesbian rights activists.

The Marrying Kind

WHEN JACK BAKER AND J. MICHAEL McCONNELL were featured as part of *Look* magazine's "The American Family" issue in January of 1971, they were "the closest things to national personalities that the gay liberation movement had produced." Baker and McConnell presented themselves as a stable, traditional alternative to the enduring stereotype of a sex-crazed, pathological male homosexual—the Minneapolis couple attended Catholic Mass together, and they actually applied for a marriage license in May 1970. Baker, a student at law school, realized that Minnesota state law didn't explicitly prohibit same-sex marriage. McConnell later stated that "We didn't apply for a marriage license because we thought it would be fun to do. We did it because we thought it would have a profound impact on this culture. The most sacred institution in our country is marriage." But their

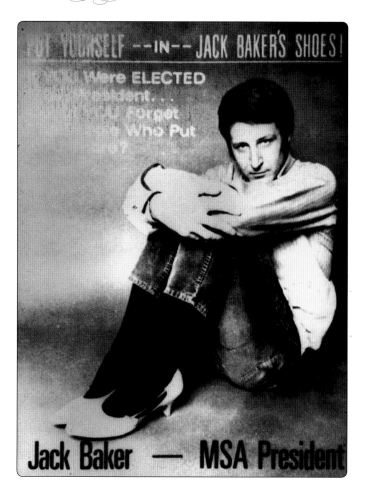

PUT YOURSELF --IN-- JACK BAKER'S SHOES!

...Were ELECTED

Jack Baker — MSA President

troubles didn't end with the city's refusal to grant the license: McConnell lost his job offer as head cataloguer at the University of Minnesota's St. Paul library branch when their case was publicized in the newspapers. Soon they were battling in court against both the city and the university for discrimination. Baker was president of the campus gay group FREE (Fight Repression of Erotic Expression), and he used the newfound media visibility of his marriage attempt to run for student body president. His campaign featured campy posters, including one picturing Baker in high heels with the tag line, "Put Yourself in Jack Baker's Shoes." He won the election in April 1971, becoming the first openly gay man to win public office. Unfortunately, the couple lost both of their legal cases under appeal. (Although in 1975, six Colorado couples were granted marriage licenses in Boulder through the same reasoning that the state had no laws dealing with the possibility. Unfortunately, the state's attorney general insisted the licenses weren't valid.)

Cured!

WITH ALL THESE WACKY YOUNG RADICALS getting all the attention, you might think the old-school activists, the homophiles, had pretty much given up what they were doing—but you would be wrong. In 1971, Franklin Kameny actually ran for Congress in Washington, D.C. He knew he wasn't going to win, but he would bring attention to homosexual issues.

Then, in 1973, the American Psychiatric Association finally declared that homosexuality per se was not a mental illness—just about one hundred years after homosexuality was first "discovered" in America, and seventeen years after Dr. Hooker's study of gay men. The change happened like this.

In 1970, the American Psychiatric Association included a program on "Issues of Sexuality" at its annual conference in San Francisco. In the middle of the discussion, several radical homosexual activists got up and demanded to be heard, insisting that it was high time for psychiatrists to listen to homosexuals telling their own story. The APA was flustered, and to avoid another outburst the next year, the conference organizers offered gay rights activists the opportunity to participate in a panel. The 1971 panel went smoothly (after activists had disrupted the former attorney general's speech at the convention the day before), but it didn't get the kind of attention the activists had hoped for. Franklin Kameny and Barbara Gittings set up an exhibit on gay issues at the conference, and there they discovered not only did many straight psychiatrists agree with their views of homosexuality but a secret, highly closeted organization of homosexual psychiatrists had existed within the APA for years (cheekily called the "Gay PA"). The activists figured that the only way they could convince the majority of the APA that the official position on homosexuality was wrong was if they could present a gay psychiatrist at next year's panel. Unfortunately, none of the gay psychiatrists Gittings talked to would risk his career by admitting his homosexuality publicly. Finally, one Philadelphia doctor agreed to appear at the presentation as "Dr. Henry Anonymous" wearing a mask and using a voice-distorting microphone. Kameny wasn't thrilled about the props, but the psychiatrist's dramatic appearance

LEFT: Franklin Kameny, the first openly homosexual candidate for United States Congress. 1971.

OPPOSITE: Campaign poster for openly homosexual Jack Baker, running for president of the University of Minnesota Student Association. 1971.

made the panel all the more effective—the presentation was packed, and the tide of opinion began to turn. By December 1973, the Board of Trustees had voted in favor of homosexuality's reclassification (a decision later confirmed by a majority vote of the membership, though hardcore anti-gay psychiatrists like Irving Bieber and Charles Socarides would continue to claim that homosexuality was some kind of a curable disorder). It wasn't until 1994 that "Dr. Anonymous" revealed himself to be a man named John Fryer.

Southern Arson

T HE SAME YEAR AS THE RECLASSIFICATION OF HOMOSEXUALITY by the APA, New Orleans experienced its worst tragedy in almost two hundred years—though relatively few took notice. The local branch of the Metropolitan Community Church (MCC) held its services in a gay bar called UpStairs in the French Quarter. (MCC founder Rev. Troy Perry was quoted as saying, "We didn't care. If Jesus could turn water into wine, hell, we could worship in a bar.") On the last Sunday in June 1973, the same day as Stonewall's fourth anniversary parade in New York, an estimated forty to sixty people were in the bar, with most of the MCC congregants present. Just before eight P.M., someone set fire to the wooden stairs leading to the second-floor front door of the bar. Then that person rang the buzzer downstairs, which was used by taxicab drivers when they were called for a pickup. When the steel door to the stairwell opened, the flames burst inside. At least ten people jumped out the windows to their deaths, while some got stuck in the windows and burned to death. Fifteen people were sent to the hospital, and twenty-nine bodies were collected—although a total of thirty-two people would eventually die from the fire.

In New Orleans, residents were embarrassed by the event because it involved homosexuals. The local press did not mention that UpStairs was a gay bar—their readership was already aware of that. But out-of-state newspapers didn't know, so their stories didn't explain the significance of the fire. No public officials would make a public statement about the event. The police determined that arson was the cause, but no one was ever charged. One burn victim, a schoolteacher, was fired while still in the hospital—two weeks before he died from his injuries. Reverend Bill Larson's mother did not want her now-publicly homosexual son buried in their hometown, nor would she accept his ashes; several families refused to claim their sons. Then, to top it off, a number of local churches refused to allow national MCC leaders to use their buildings for a mourning service.

Progress

BUT DESPITE SUCH HARROWING TRAGEDIES, the 1970s were a relatively good decade for the gay rights movement. Success just seemed to follow success. Gay rights activists were finding more and more supporters among straight politicians, most notably New York City Congresswoman Bella Abzug and San Francisco's State Assemblyman Willie Brown. The Alice B. Toklas Memorial Democratic Club, a San Francisco gay political club, organized the much-wooed gay voting bloc in the city and helped arrange speakers at the national Democratic convention in 1972. In 1973, the National Gay Task Force (NGTF, later called the National Gay and Lesbian Task Force, NGLTF) was formed as a truly national gay rights organization. Despite its shoestring budget, the NGTF was instrumental in getting the U.S. Civil Service Commission to stop excluding homosexuals from federal employment in 1975, and it helped make gay rights an official priority of the Democratic Party during the 1976 and 1980 national conventions. Activists even nominated a gay vice presidential candidate, Melvin Boozer, for the Democratic Party at the 1980 convention. In 1975, Elaine Noble, elected to office in the Massachusetts House of Representatives, was the first openly homosexual

RIGHT: Bella Abzug at the 1972 Miami Democratic National Convention. July 1972.

OPPOSITE: Barbara Gittings, Franklin Kameny, "Dr. Henry Anonymous," and Dr. Judd Marmor (from left to right) at the May 1972 American Psychiatric Association convention.

American political figure Midge Costanza, aide to President Jimmy Carter, 1970s. Called "the President's window to the nation," Costanza consulted with a wide array of groups—among the first was a delegation of gay and lesbian leaders.

legislator. In San Francisco, a young gay camera shop owner named Harvey Milk won a seat on the Board of Supervisors in 1977. In March of that same year, gay rights leaders were even invited to the White House for a meeting with President Jimmy Carter's public liaison, Midge Costanza.

But with all these victories came a certain laziness about political action among gays and lesbians. Morty Manford, an early GAA member, later blamed "the general dissipation of the Left, which really had been held together by the antiwar movement. People were becoming more self-centered. . . . I suppose that people had become tired of all the activism and the confrontation tactics as a means of dealing with problems." Gay rights groups began having trouble getting people to go to demonstrations and protests. Things seemed to be going in the right direction, anyway—sodomy laws were being repealed all over, and nondiscrimination laws were passed in more than forty cities to protect sexual orientation. And really, who can be bothered when there's disco to dance to?

Shake Your Groove Thing

IT'S TRUE—A LOT OF THE REASON POLITICAL ACTIVISM was waning among gay men in the late 1970s was because while many continued to fight for their rights, many others were too drugged out and having wild sex to even think about politics. A lot of gay men took to their new police-harassment-free social lives like ducks to water. The Mafia bars were quickly forgotten as newer, bigger, cooler discotheques and sex palaces opened up. The Continental Baths, the Mineshaft, the Anvil in Manhattan, and the elaborate bathhouses of San Francisco—every major city soon had establishments that were notorious for anonymous sex and S&M leather culture. Party drugs like speed, barbiturates, and cocaine became fashionable at discos, with Studio 54 famously featuring an image of the Man in the Moon with an animated coke spoon.

High on their newfound freedom, gay men resented anyone who criticized their party lifestyle. After a gay Hollywood screenwriter named Larry Kramer published his first novel, *Faggots*, in 1978, in which he depicted (and deplored) the sex and drug use rampant among high-flying gay men in New York, he complained that "people literally crossed the street not to talk to me. My best friend stopped talking to me. . . . When I went to Fire Island for the first time after the book came out, I was shunned." William Friedkin's movie *Cruising*, released in early 1980, was protested all throughout its filming because activists had learned that it depicted gay nightlife in a negative light.

For many, this new level of sexuality was an exciting adventure. One clubgoer recalled a club on Fire Island, saying it was "the most fabulous disco I'd ever been to in my life because there were two thousand writhing, drugged, beautiful bodies dancing on this dance floor. By six a.m., we were outside around the pool, and we were dancing under the stars as the sun was coming up. And I believed at that moment in time that we were having more fun than anybody in the history of civilization had ever had." In the view of many gay men, they were figuring out new ways to live that didn't center on monogamy. They didn't have much reason *not* to have a lot of sex—while American culture looked down on

Dance club Studio 54 in New York. Early 1980s.

Portrait of the original members of the American disco group the Village People. 1977.

sexually active women, sexually active men never faced the same kind of disapproval. With a gay encounter, there was no risk of pregnancy, and most sexually transmitted diseases at the time were easily treatable. The *last* thing many gay men wanted was something as stable and boringly heterosexual as marriage—they believed they were creating an exciting, sexually adventurous new way to live life.

Disco's energy was infectious, and soon it began to seep into the mainstream. Gay discos became known as glam hot spots to be seen, and straights were soon begging their gay friends to take them along. In 1977, the disco film classic *Saturday Night Fever* ignored the scene's gay vibe, and homoerotically charged songs like the Village Peoples' 1978 ode to the YMCA (a known cruising ground for gays since at least World War I) soon became staples of family wedding parties.

But that was all right, this was a totally new era for gay people—by 1977 you could turn on your TV to see Billy Crystal playing the first gay character in a television series on *Soap*. Gays and lesbians could see that they were finally on track to getting the rights and recognition they deserved.

A Wicked Queen

AND THEN CAME THE FLORIDA BEAUTY QUEEN. In 1977, Anita Bryant, onetime Miss Oklahoma and gold-record singer best known for her commercials for Florida orange juice, became incensed when Dade County passed a nondiscrimination bill protecting homosexuals. Bryant, a devoted member of the Northwest Baptist Church, got it into her head that the new law "condones immorality and discriminates against my children's rights to grow up in a healthy, decent community." A group of conservative political strategists and religious leaders gathered around her to form Save Our Children, Inc., an organization that soon led a successful petition drive to hold a

LEFT: A participant in the Gay Freedom Day parade in San Francisco holds a sign protesting Anita Bryant and her antigay Save Our Children campaign. June 26, 1977.

ABOVE: Anita Bryant, once a popular hit singer in the early 1960s, became known as an outspoken opponent of gay rights. May 1977.

referendum election on the new ordinance. The campaign was brutal: Save Our Children promoted the phrase "Homosexuals cannot reproduce, so they must recruit," in effect accusing homosexuals of being child molesters. Bryant published a book, *The Anita Bryant Story: The Survival of Our Nation's Families and the Threat of Militant Homosexuality*, and she announced plans to open counseling centers across the country that would "convert" homosexuals to heterosexuals. The rhetoric was effective: the ordinance was repealed in a landslide victory. Similar laws were soon struck down in St. Paul, Minnesota; Wichita, Kansas; and Eugene, Oregon—and Oklahoma even passed a law banning homosexuals from teaching in public schools.

Organized homosexuals had their first organized enemy, a movement that burst out of social conservatives' simmering resentment of all the gains homosexuals had made in the last several years. Thankfully, the disturbing things said and done by the evangelical right shook up the gay and lesbian community, and the pride parades of 1977 saw record numbers of participants—with 250,000 marching in San Francisco alone—and gays and lesbians across the nation began boycotting Florida

Supervisor Harvey Milk (left) and Mayor George Moscone of San Francisco shake hands as the mayor signs a gay rights ordinance. April 1978.

orange juice. In California, a state senator named John Briggs put together a referendum on whether homosexuals could teach in public schools. Following Bryant's kooky line of reasoning, Briggs stated, "Homosexuals want your children. They don't have any children of their own. If they don't recruit children or very young people, they'd all die away. They have no means of replenishing. That's why they want to be teachers." Fortunately, the Briggs Initiative, aka Proposition 6, was soundly defeated in November 1978—though many credit the victory to former California governor Ronald Reagan, who observed, "Whatever else it is, homosexuality is not a contagious disease like measles." Meanwhile, in Seattle, a Bryant-like attempt to repeal the city's gay rights law (initiated by a group called Save Our Moral Ethics) was also shot down.

Assassinations

DESPITE THE ELECTORAL SUCCESS, that same month, November 1978, would be remembered as a tragic one in San Francisco. Harvey Milk, the gay city supervisor from the gay neighborhood of the Castro, found himself working alongside another supervisor, Dan White, a working-class Catholic man who was outspoken about his conservative values. Ten days after White suddenly resigned his position (because of his financial situation, he said), he asked Mayor George Moscone to reinstate him. White's political enemies (Milk included) blocked the reappointment, and on a Monday morning in late November, White snuck into City Hall through a window, walked into Mayor Moscone's office, and shot him dead. He then took Milk to his former office and shot him dead, too.

Dan White's trial for murder was a travesty: the jury selection was questionable, the prosecution did a sloppy job, and the defense argued that White's antisocial behavior was caused by eating lots of junk food—this became known as the "Twinkie defense." The jury decided that White was guilty of only two counts of voluntary manslaughter, and he was sentenced to seven years and eight months of hard time—he would likely be out in five years. That night, May 21, 1979, thousands of angry protesters converged on City Hall and trashed a dozen police cars. The police struck back, attacking randomly in Castro's streets—sixty-one police officers and one hundred gays were hospitalized for what would become known as the "White Night Riots."

Aftermath

BRYANT AND WHITE DIDN'T LAST LONG in the spotlight. Bryant faced gay rights protesters for a few years at her public events, and she stopped receiving invitations to speak and perform. The Florida Citrus Commission decided that she was too controversial, and they didn't extend her contract. She eventually filed for bankruptcy. White got out of the slammer in 1985, and he, too, was unable to find work. He committed suicide within a year.

Meanwhile, Harvey Milk's death became a rallying symbol for the gay rights movement, a martyrdom that gave new energy and purpose to the cause. In 1979, activists held the first March on Washington for Lesbian and Gay Rights, drawing one hundred thousand participants. Randy Shilts published a popular biography of the "Mayor of Castro Street" in 1982, and in 1984, the documentary film *The Life and Times of Harvey Milk* won an Academy Award.

Nevertheless, Bryant's crusade had sparked the Christian evangelical right into building itself up as a formidable enemy to the progress of gay rights.

But nothing could compare to the terror that waited in the shadows.

Mourners hold a candlelight vigil for Mayor George Moscone and Supervisor Harvey Milk after they were assassinated at City Hall. November 27, 1978.

"Our continued existence as gay men upon the face of this earth is at stake. Unless we fight for our lives, we shall die. In all the history of homosexuality we have never before been so close to death and extinction. Many of us are dying or already dead."

—LARRY KRAMER, "1,112 AND COUNTING," MARCH 1983

Your Hometown, USA, 1980

YOUR BEST FRIEND GETS SICK. He's always tired. Then he starts feeling nauseous all the time. He has a high fever. He's losing too much weight. He has severe diarrhea.

Of course, he goes to his doctor. She doesn't know what's wrong with him. She recommends another doctor. Who recommends another doctor. Who recommends another. No one can figure out how he got sick, or even what's wrong with him.

Maybe he has white fungus growing around his fingernails. Maybe he has large purple bumps all over his skin. Maybe he goes completely blind and, worse, starts losing his mind.

He has tried everything and anything. What little money he has left he spends on "miracle" vitamin supplements. He takes up meditation.

But too quickly, he dies a horrible death, say, by suffocating from a microscopic fungus filling his lungs.

Every morning, you check yourself for bumps in the shower.

The gay newspaper *New York Native* published the first article about the disease that later became known as AIDS and then continued to cover the epidemic in far more detail than the mainstream news media.

Then another friend tells you he has begun feeling tired all the time. More and more of your friends get sick. You find it harder to keep up with your work. You spend all your time visiting ailing friends at their homes, bringing them food, cleaning up the diarrhea and vomit, paying their bills, and rushing them to the hospital.

You're tired of organizing their funerals.

But is that the only reason you're tired? Perhaps you really are next.

And worst of all, no one seems to care.

In fact, some people tell you that you and your friends all *deserve* to die.

ABOVE: Larry Kramer—author, AIDS campaigner, and gay rights activist—is a founder of ACT UP and the Gay Men's Health Crisis group. December 20, 1988.

OPPOSITE: Dr. Robert Gallo, head of the Tumor Cell Biology Laboratory at the National Cancer Institute and Health and Human Services Secretary Margaret Heckler hold a press conference concerning the cause of Acquired Immune Deficiency Syndrome (AIDS). Washington, D.C. April 23, 1984.

Kramer vs. AIDS

WHEN AMERICANS FIRST BEGAN GETTING SICK from AIDS around 1980, no one could understand what was going on—there was only horror.

By the summer of 1981, three of Larry Kramer's friends had suddenly died from strange, terrifying illnesses, and he knew something terrible was going on in the gay community. Kramer contacted Dr. Alvin Friedman-Kien, coauthor of the first published report on what would become known as AIDS, and he told Kramer that he suspected the cause to be something sexually transmitted. Meanwhile, rumors started circulating among gay New Yorkers of a new "gay cancer." Sometimes the illness was called "Saint's disease" because several of the earliest patients were regulars at the Saint, one of Manhattan's hottest gay clubs. Kramer wrote editorial letters to the *New York Native*, a gay New York newspaper, begging gay men to curb their sex lives until scientists determined once and for all what was causing this thing. In August 1981, he invited about eighty gay men to his apartment, where Friedman-Kien presented disturbing statistics about the rising number of sick men. Six months later, Kramer and his friends started Gay Men's Health Crisis (GMHC), an organization that would become the leading AIDS services organization in the country. But in 1981 and 1982, Larry Kramer was still known as the man who wrote *Faggots*, a novel criticizing the gay sex-and-drugs party lifestyle in New York. Very few gay men were interested in hearing about some weird cancer that Kramer claimed was caused by their wild sex.

But by March 1983, when the *New York Native* published Kramer's essay, "1,112 and Counting," gay men couldn't help but pay attention. Kramer listed twenty-one people whom he had known who were dead because of AIDS. A total of 428 Americans had died in just a couple years. The essay went to town on how AIDS was being ignored by the media and the mayor, how research and funding were being delayed by the federal government, and how even the gay community was dragging its feet in recognizing the problem and doing something about it. On all counts, he was right.

The Sickness That Dares Not Speak Its Name

AT FIRST, THERE WAS SO MUCH CONFUSION surrounding the disease: what was causing it, how to test for it, and what could be done about it. Described as a "rare cancer" in the very first Centers for Disease Control (CDC) report in 1981, the mysterious illness was named GRID (Gay-Related Immune Deficiency). After reports surfaced that some heterosexual hemophiliacs, drug addicts, and Haitians had been diagnosed with the disease, the name was changed in 1982 to Acquired Immune Deficiency Syndrome (AIDS). Patients with AIDS frequently had Kaposi's Sarcoma (KS), a rare type of cancer that causes purple lumps to appear on the skin. KS was thought to affect only older Italian and Jewish men, who rarely ever died from it. Many AIDS patients also succumbed to *Pneumocystis jiroveci*, a tiny organism that can fill up a person's lungs when the immune system is shot. Others were dying from toxoplasmosis (a disease caused by a parasite often found in cat feces), a sheep-bowel parasite called *Cryptosporidium*, and the *Cryptococcus* parasite found in bird feces.

The cause of AIDS took a long time to discover. Initially, doctors suspected a variety of possibilities, from too many traditional sexually transmitted diseases crashing the immune system to the "poppers" that many gay men inhaled at clubs to get high. Less reputable experts had different ideas: a psychologist in the San Francisco area published a series of articles arguing that AIDS was due to psychological traumas from childhood. One supermarket tabloid claimed that AIDS was a curse from King Tut—a traveling exhibition in the late '70s had displayed the ancient treasures found in his tomb. Meanwhile, terrified gay men turned to all kinds of crazy stuff to try to protect themselves, including a variety of fraudulent diet therapies and expensive so-called "vitamin packets" that were advertised in gay newspapers. Federal postal inspectors shut down one company that claimed their mail-order injection could cure AIDS—for a cool $1,900.

Finally, in 1984, the National Institutes of Health declared the "probable cause" of AIDS to be a virus, calling it "HTLV-III." Later it became clear that French scientists at the Pasteur Institute had discovered it a year before and had named it "LAV." (The French had to go so far as to sue the National Cancer Institute for recognition until an international committee finally ruled in favor of the French in 1986—but the committee settled on a compromise to call it the Human Immunodeficiency Virus, HIV.) So, scientists finally figured out what caused AIDS, but there was no test available for HIV until March 1985. By then, more than 4,300 people had died.

The Facts

THESE ARE THE FACTS: AIDS is a breakdown of the body's immune system, leaving the body vulnerable to any number of infections that would be harmless to a healthy person. AIDS is caused by the HIV virus, which can be found in bodily fluids such as blood and semen, and it is most often transmitted in three ways: unprotected sex, sharing used needles, and being born from an HIV-positive mother. Though the earliest confirmed case of HIV has been traced to a Congolese man in 1959, there is a lot of disagreement as to when humans first became infected with HIV—some experts even suggest the nineteenth century. The disease has since exploded all over the world, especially within the continental African population, and it has become a crisis of staggering proportions.

AIDS became famously associated with gay men in the early 1980s because they were the first population in America to notice its effects—the common practice among gay men of unprotected anal sex was a relatively efficient way of spreading the virus. Throughout the 1980s and beyond, the history of AIDS became inseparable from the history of the gay and lesbian community.

Because of the rapid spread of AIDS, city officials closed sex clubs known to be frequented by gay men, such as the Mineshaft Bar in New York City. November 12, 1985.

Deathhouses

THE SPEED OF THE SPREAD of the virus was helped in no small part by the hypersexuality found at bathhouses in America's major cities. Specifically gay bathhouses had been a fixture of American cities since at least the early 1900s, and the sexual revolution of the 1970s only expanded this traditional aspect of gay urban life to a candy land of sexual possibilities. The new baths often included disco music, free alcohol, a variety of drugs, anonymous sex, and group orgies. The largest bathhouse in San Francisco, the Bulldog Baths, was built to imitate San Quentin prison, complete with barred cells and "guards." In one pre-1980 study of Denver bathhouses, the average attendee clocked 2.7 sexual contacts a night. At the time, almost all gay men didn't even *consider* using a condom for sex, since pregnancy wasn't a risk and sexually transmitted diseases could usually be cleared up with a quick trip to the doctor.

Hundreds of these establishments across the United States and Canada constituted a $100 million industry. Many bath owners were prominent activists and vital financial supporters of gay organizations and gay news magazines—including, ironically, the growing number of AIDS support groups that were forming.

Dr. Mervyn Silverman, the director of health for the city and county of San Francisco, displays a poster and leaflets meant to educate people to the health risks posed by Acquired Immune Deficiency Syndrome,

In San Francisco, Larry Littlejohn was a fixture of gay activism; he had been president of the Society for Individual Rights (SIR) in the 1960s. But when Littlejohn read Kramer's "1,112 and Counting" in 1983, he concluded that the city's baths represented a clear public health danger. Littlejohn began campaigning to have the city close them down, and was surprised to discover how sensitive the subject was: He and his supporters came to be *hated* by many San Franciscans. Some gay leaders proclaimed that closing bathhouses was the first step toward forced concentration camps for all gays.

After a drawn-out political fight within the gay community, city public health director Mervyn Silverman finally closed the baths in October 1984. In New York, the baths and sex clubs like the Mineshaft Bar were shut down in 1985—over the objections of AIDS activists, many of whom believed that these places represented ideal opportunities for public health education efforts. Larry Kramer later remembered, "Oh, God, the battle over whether or not to close the baths became such a red herring because of this issue of sexual freedom. It took all our energy, and it took all our fighting. It shouldn't have been an issue, period!"

If You Prick Us, Do We Not Bleed?

THEN THERE WAS THE BLOOD SCREENING ISSUE. Gay men were traditionally very reliable blood donors, and the blood industry didn't want to cause a panic about its stocks of donated blood. In 1983, the FDA recommended excluding potential donors who were "at increased risk," which meant all men who had had sex with another man since 1977. Many gay rights advocates were alarmed by the restriction, and they demonstrated. Others welcomed the change, believing it would save lives in the long run. In 1985, the year all donated blood began to be screened with a test, the risk of HIV infection by blood was one in 2,500. (Today it is less than one in a million.) By that time, more than six thousand people had been infected through donated blood (including almost two thousand hemophiliacs who relied on blood-clotting factors extracted from blood).

Uncle Sam Doesn't Care

MEANWHILE, THE FEDERAL GOVERNMENT was doing very little in response to the rapid spread of AIDS. Although the CDC had described the disease as an "epidemic" as early as 1981, President Ronald Reagan refused to provide adequate funding for dealing with the disease. In fact, he *didn't even say the word* "AIDS" in public until 1986, and his first major speech to mention AIDS was in 1987—when almost 21,000 people had already died from it. Secretary Margaret Heckler of the U.S. Department of Health and Human Services kept telling the media that her department had everything under control, that they didn't need any more money—but researchers were actually

begging, borrowing, and stealing from other programs in order to fund AIDS research efforts. Congress had to pass laws to force the federal government to direct more funding toward AIDS research. The lack of coverage by the news media didn't help matters, either—discussing gay people and sexual disease made both readers and journalists squeamish.

Some Christian evangelicals with a great deal of influence in Washington weren't helping matters by saying that gay men deserved to die from AIDS. Rev. Jerry Falwell, founder of the Moral Majority political action group, said, "AIDS is the wrath of God upon homosexuals." Reagan's own communications director (and later presidential hopeful) Pat Buchanan stated that AIDS was "nature's revenge on gay men." In 1987, America watched on national TV as AIDS activists outside the White House were arrested by policemen wearing rubber gloves—long after it had been established that HIV could not be transmitted through casual contact. Rabidly homophobic North Carolina Senator Jesse Helms amended a federal appropriations bill to prohibit AIDS education efforts that "encourage or promote homosexual activity," basically rendering those efforts useless because organizations were prevented from explaining safe sex to gay men. Helms also made sure people living with HIV were excluded from entering the United States.

Of course, there were some people in the government who were doing whatever they could to help, like the struggling, underfinanced researchers at the CDC. Surgeon General C. Everett Koop took a politically brave stand in 1986 by recommending an aggressive education program for youth: "Education about AIDS should start at an early age so that children can grow up knowing the behaviors to avoid to protect themselves from exposure to the AIDS virus." Then, in 1988, the Presidential Commission on HIV, headed by Admiral James Watkins, recommended laws that prohibited discrimination against people with AIDS and encouraged AIDS education as early as kindergarten. The recommendations were largely ignored.

Freakin'

DURING THE BATHHOUSE controversy, gay men hadn't been totally nuts by being worried about being rounded up—the American public was just starting to freak out about AIDS. Stories started circulating about nurses and orderlies who refused to take care of AIDS patients. Police in San Francisco were given surgical masks and gloves to wear when dealing with "suspected AIDS patients." There were also reports of landlords evicting AIDS patients and Social Security Administration workers interviewing patients over the phone rather than in person. A group called Dallas Doctors Against AIDS distributed pamphlets that read, "Such a severe public health concern

ABOVE: A protester is handcuffed by a policeman wearing protective rubber gloves during a demonstration calling for a "Medical Manhattan Project on AIDS" in front of the White House. Police believed the gloves would protect them from AIDS patients who were participating in the protest. June 1, 1987.

OPPOSITE: President Reagan chats with Moral Majority leader Rev. Jerry Falwell at the White House. July 12, 1983.

must cause the citizenry of this country to do everything in their power to smash the homosexual movement in this country to make sure these kinds of acts are criminalized." Polls from 1985 showed that 72 percent of Americans supported mandatory testing, 51 percent were OK with keeping HIV patients under quarantine, and 15 percent even favored tattooing them for identification! Thirteen-year-old (hemophiliac) Ryan White was barred from going to school because he had contracted HIV through a blood transfusion. The Justice Department ruled that people suspected of having HIV could be legally fired. Also, twenty states introduced bills to ban AIDS patients from food-handling and educational jobs, to make it a crime to transmit HIV, and to force testing of prostitutes. A few of those laws actually passed, but thankfully in 1986 Californians soundly rejected a state initiative proposed by a political extremist named Lyndon LaRouche to actually *quarantine* people living with AIDS.

The AIDS crisis quickly highlighted how vulnerable gay men were in a legal sense. Many partners of gay men discovered that they could be barred from visiting their dying lovers in hospitals, since they were not considered family members. And after many men died, their partners were kept from accessing their rightful inheritances by long-estranged families that disapproved of homosexuality. Without the legal protections of marriage, many gay men were being kicked while they were already down.

Sisters Are Doin' It for Themselves

BOTH IGNORED AND ANTAGONIZED from the start of the AIDS crisis, the gay community realized pretty early on that if progress was going to be made, it would have to come from their own. As historian Charles Kaiser described it, "The disease would convert a generation of mostly selfish men, consumed by sex, into a highly disciplined army of fearless and selfless street fighters and caregivers." In New York, Gay Men's Health Crisis was providing care for two hundred fifty people with the help of five hundred volunteers by the end of 1983—it had grown to be the largest gay organization in the country. The group developed an innovative Buddy Program to help AIDS patients with everyday needs, lobbied the government for AIDS funding, battled discrimination against people with HIV/AIDS, and worked to educate gay men about risky behavior. In 1982, the organization started the first AIDS hotline (aka volunteer Rodger McFarlane's answering machine), which received more than one hundred calls on just the first night.

Other early voluntary organizations included AIDS Project Los Angeles (APLA) and the San Francisco AIDS Foundation (SFAF). Actually, in San Francisco, the community was better organized to deal with the epidemic than New York, since the city itself was putting money into creating special

AIDS wards, patient support programs, grief counseling, and education efforts. Journalist Randy Shilts calculated that the city and county of San Francisco's spending on AIDS in 1982 was 20 percent of the total spending on the disease in the United States.

Gay and lesbian rights activists essentially dropped their political plans and focused on this new threat. From the very start of the AIDS epidemic, lesbians largely put aside their own pressing agenda and rushed to aid their dying friends, and the epidemic brought gays and lesbians together in a powerful way. True, the antigay backlash affected lesbians, too, but their work was borne out of compassion more than anything. They reliably gave blood, volunteered at AIDS service organizations, led protests, and filled the increasing number of vacancies in gay organizations—all despite the fact that statistically they had the lowest AIDS infection rates. Which, of course, made the Rev. Jerry Falwell's comment that God was punishing gay men with AIDS particularly ironic—as historian Lillian Faderman pointed out, would that make lesbians "God's elect"?

Actor Rock Hudson. 1950s.

Fame!

TRUTHFULLY, IT WASN'T UNTIL ROCK HUDSON DIED in July of 1985 that AIDS really got the attention of mainstream America. Rock Hudson was a beloved Hollywood movie star (and closeted gay man) who had made more than seventy movies during three decades. Just before visiting Ronald and Nancy Reagan (old Hollywood friends) at the White House in the summer of 1984, Hudson flew to Paris to receive the latest AIDS treatments. But even after it was revealed that

Actress Elizabeth Taylor testifying on the need for AIDS research before the Senate Appropriations Labor and Health Subcommittee. Washington, D.C., May 1986.

Hudson was dead because of AIDS, the Reagans kept up their awful silence.

Meanwhile, another of Hudson's famous friends, legendary screen actress Elizabeth Taylor, responded very differently to the AIDS crisis. In 1985, she lent her star power to fund-raising efforts by AIDS Project Los Angeles. She then cofounded a foundation eventually known as amFAR (the American Foundation for AIDS Research), and by 1991 had established another AIDS foundation bearing her name. Similarly, British pop singer Elton John participated in mid-1980s fund-raisers, befriended Indiana teenager Ryan White before his tragic death in 1990, and started the Elton John AIDS Foundation in 1992. Other early celebrity fund-raisers included Debbie Reynolds, Sammy Davis Jr., Morgan Fairchild, and Shirley MacLaine. These high-profile celebrity actions had a snowball effect; amFAR's national council soon included Barbra Streisand, Woody Allen, and Warren Beatty. In 1985, Dionne Warwick released a version of "That's What Friends Are For" with Stevie Wonder, Gladys Knight, and Elton John to raise money for amFAR. Other celebrities increasingly lent their support, but it wasn't until the early nineties that *everyone* was willing to do something like wear red AIDS ribbons at public events—in the mid-'80s, AIDS was just too controversial because of its association with gay men. The public support shown by some celebrities was an important contribution to the evolving views of the American public regarding AIDS.

Double Smackdown

IN 1986, THE GAY AND LESBIAN CIVIL RIGHTS MOVEMENT in America experienced two blows. The first came from the Vatican, which issued a statement (penned by Cardinal Ratzinger, later to become Pope Benedict XVI) to Roman Catholic bishops describing homosexuality as "a tendency ordered toward an intrinsic moral evil." Furthermore, the letter ordered church officials to withdraw all support from gay Catholic organizations such as Dignity, which had been founded in 1969 and had some six thousand members across America. Gays and lesbians were stunned by the lack of compassion, particularly at the height of the AIDS crisis.

The second blow came from the United States Supreme Court in the case of *Bowers v. Hardwick.* Back in 1982, a policeman had arrested Michael Hardwick on a charge of "sodomy"—unlike many other states, Georgia had never repealed its colonial-era sodomy laws. (The policeman had come into Hardwick's home to serve a warrant, and he found Hardwick engaged in oral sex.) The case was appealed all the way up to the Supreme Court, where activists hoped the court would rule in favor of Hardwick, thereby nullifying all the remaining sodomy laws in the United States and removing the basis for many other discriminatory laws.

But no.

The court came back with a 5–4 verdict *against* Hardwick, claiming "millennia of moral teaching" as justification, among other things. Justice Lewis Powell later said that he had "probably made a mistake" in voting against Hardwick—but for the next ten years, private consensual gay sex would remain illegal in some states.

Ryan White, an Indiana teenager who contracted AIDS through blood transfusions, returns to the school that he was barred from because of his disease. April 10, 1986. He died in 1990.

Rage Against the Machine

EVEN THOUGH HE WAS THE LEAD FOUNDER of the organization, Larry Kramer didn't last very long at Gay Men's Health Crisis. He was so bitter and argumentative, no one would elect him to a leadership position. Kramer battled GMHC from within for a while, arguing that the organization should be more aggressive in telling gay men to stop having unsafe sex. Better yet, he thought GMHC should be telling gay men to stop having sex altogether—their lives depended on it. Why wasn't the organization kicking and screaming, confronting the mayor on the lack of a citywide AIDS response?

Eventually, in 1983, Kramer quit GMHC out of frustration.

Four years later, gays and lesbians had reached a boiling point. After six years of battling for attention, funding, and basic human decency, many activist gays and lesbians were getting frustrated with the traditional ways of getting things done. They were tired of countless meetings with officials that went nowhere, tired of approval delays for experimental drugs, tired of seeing rising violence against gays, and most of all, they were tired of burying their friends. In spring of 1986 the National Cancer Institute had announced that a drug called zidovudine, more commonly known as AZT, showed some promise in treating people with AIDS, but it wasn't generally available until the FDA approved it a year later. When it came out, the drug cost about $10,000 for a year's supply, making it one of the most expensive medications ever sold.

In December 1986, a hairstylist named Avram Finkelstein and a group of his friends designed and posted stark "Silence = Death" posters all over New York, and the image fast became the icon of AIDS activism. Then a very small group of radicals calling themselves the Lavender Hill Mob started mounting GAA-style media zaps in February 1987 to protest the sluggish medical bureaucracy and the dire lack of funding. The anger was out there; it just needed to be organized in a big way.

In March 1987, Kramer was featured as the weekly speaker at New York's Lesbian and Gay

LEFT: In December 1989, more than five thousand ACT UP demonstrators protested in front of St. Patrick's Cathedral in midtown Manhattan against Cardinal John O'Connor and the Catholic Archdiocese.

OPPOSITE, TOP: The Silence = Death image became a leading icon of AIDS activism. 1986.

OPPOSITE, BOTTOM: Members of the gay Catholic group Dignity form a human cross in front of St Patrick's Cathedral on Fifth Avenue in New York City, protesting their expulsion from an archdiocese church where they had been holding masses. March 6, 1988.

Community Center. There he gave a speech in which he had two-thirds of the room stand, telling them, "You could be dead in less than five years." His speech inspired three hundred people to gather two days later and form a group later known as ACT UP, which stands for "AIDS Coalition to Unleash Power." These men and women were the next generation of gay radicals, and their anger would prove to be quite powerful. They described themselves as "united in anger and committed to direct action to end the AIDS crisis." They had the anger of the Gay Liberation Front and the creativity of Gay Activists Alliance—and they were ready to start some trouble.

The group decided its first goal would be the early release of all experimental drugs that could treat AIDS. When pharmaceutical giant Burroughs Wellcome announced sky-high prices for AZT, ACT UP activists descended on Wall Street. They sat down in the middle of rush-hour traffic, bringing all of lower Manhattan to a complete standstill. Later protests would include throwing fake money onto the floor of the New York Stock Exchange and having "Die-Ins" along Wall Street. When Northwest Airlines decided to deny tickets to people with AIDS, ACT UP flooded the airline with false reservations. They threw buckets of fake blood into public places, screaming that it was "AIDS blood." At the headquarters for the Food and Drug Administration in Rockville, Maryland, one thousand people held a protest over a nine-hour period.

ACT UP's most controversial protest was held in December 1989, during Sunday Mass at St. Patrick's Cathedral in New York. Protesters entered the church, lay down in aisles, and handcuffed themselves to the pews. Forty-three people were arrested inside, and sixty-nine others were arrested outside. Many of the ACT UP protesters were themselves very ill, and deputy police commissioner Alice McGillion recalled that "Some of the protesters were taken out on orange stretchers, and they were so frail, I could have picked them up myself. It was just one of the saddest things I've ever seen." Naturally, Catholics everywhere became furious that the protest disrupted a sacramental rite. Much of the media coverage focused on an alleged incident in which one of the protesters was said to have received communion, which he then spat onto the floor—although ACT UP maintained that the organization never supported any such action.

Sex Wars: The Libido Strikes Back

ABOVE: Author Rita Mae Brown. October 1, 1977.

OPPOSITE: Actor Al Pacino in *Cruising*. 1980.

WHILE THEY WERE HELPING in the fight against AIDS, lesbians were also involved in a heated internal debate during the 1980s that became known as the "sex wars." In 1975, author/activist Rita Mae Brown had written an essay complaining about how lesbians didn't have casual sex opportunities. She wrote, "I want the option of random sex with no emotional commitment when I need sheer physical relief. . . . Like men we should have choices: deep, long-term relationships, the baths, short-term affairs." Studies during the late 1970s and early 1980s indeed showed that lesbians had less sex than either gay male or heterosexual couples. But a growing group of lesbians wanted to change that, and several started up lesbian sex businesses in the early 1980s involving pornographic videos and magazines, sadism/masochism (S&M) paraphernalia, new stores for female sex toys, female-only strip shows, and sex magazines like *On Our Backs* and *Bad Attitude*. There was also renewed interest in butch/femme roles for their overt sexuality—but this time, the roles were less clearly defined. These new interpretations of butch/femme culture were sometimes called "neo-butch" or "neo-femme"; as Daughters of Bilitis founder Phyllis Lyon noted, "women 'play at it' rather than 'being it.'"

Not surprisingly, many lesbian feminists were horrified by what they saw as attempts to imitate a kind of sexuality that reinforced males' power and put women into so-called "submissive" roles. They pressured lesbian-feminist music festivals to ban S&M seminars, pornography, and sex toys by adopting so-called pro-healing policies or a "code of feminist ethics and morality." Festival organizers often complied; otherwise, they saw the attendance drop by as much as half.

Truthfully, most lesbians weren't drawn to the new focus on in-your-face sexuality and the whole debate faded after a few years, perhaps because the effects of AIDS made sexual experimentation seem a bit scary. The 1980s were a pretty conservative decade, and dreams of a radical Lesbian Nation faded as more and more lesbians began starting their own families through artificial insemination and leading traditional, middle-class lives. Even the crunchy Olivia Records company had shifted gears by the end of the '80s and started organizing Caribbean cruises for lesbians instead.

Let Me Entertain You

THROUGHOUT THE 1980s, gays and lesbians didn't get fair treatment in mainstream entertainment. The decade started off with the release of *Cruising* in 1980, a dark film in which Al Pacino portrayed an undercover cop navigating the extremes of the gay underworld in New York. The movie was protested by gay activists throughout filming, and it ended up being a complete box-office bomb. Luckily, the controversy surrounding the film's homophobic portrayals showed moviemakers that they needed to be careful about employing negative

gay stereotypes. In 1981, Vito Russo's *The Celluloid Closet* was published, a book that criticized Hollywood's long history of antigay portrayals. But even though Billy Crystal had already played a gay character in a TV series called *Soap* in 1977, Tony Randall's character in the TV series *Love, Sidney* was stripped of his gayness in 1981 when religious groups complained.

Filmmakers tried to turn things around in 1982, when actors Harry Hamlin and Michael Ontkean starred in *Making Love*, a groundbreaking movie about a homosexual relationship that (gasp!) didn't end in tragedy. The film didn't do very well, and was almost immediately forgotten, but the number of gay characters in movies slowly began to increase. Then, in 1985, William Hurt won an Oscar for his performance in *Kiss of the Spider Woman*, which has been described as the "first truly positive portrayal of a gay man to come out of Hollywood." Not long after Rock Hudson's death, NBC aired *An Early Frost* on November 11, 1985. This TV movie was about a young man who returns home to announce his homosexuality and his AIDS diagnosis. It was a critical success, but the network lost money on the project, since advertisers were still wary of being associated with the topic.

Things were a bit better for gays on Broadway, where Harvey Fierstein's 1983 Tony–winning play *Torch Song Trilogy* was one of the first successful plays to portray a happy gay relationship. Two years later, Larry Kramer's *The Normal Heart* opened, the first AIDS-related play; many more would follow.

TOP: American playwright and actor Harvey Fierstein. Early 1980s.

LEFT: Billie Jean King returns a shot against Bobby Riggs during the Battle of the Sexes Challenge Match at the Astrodome in Houston, Texas. September 20, 1973.

OPPOSITE: Two-time Los Angeles gold medalist Greg Louganis of the United States stands on the podium after winning the Olympic springboard competition. Seoul, South Korea, 1988.

Getting a Sporting Chance

ESBIANS AND GAYS had long been invisible in the world of sports, and few in the '80s were willing to come out voluntarily. True, NFL running back David Kopay bravely announced in 1975 he was gay, after his retirement (and thereafter was denied coaching opportunities), but otherwise no one dared reveal his or her sexual orientation. Then, in 1981, tennis legend Billie Jean King was publicly outed by her former lover. King is the only woman who has won U.S. singles titles on all four surfaces (grass, clay, carpet, and hard), and she won a record twenty Wimbledon titles and thirteen U.S. Open championships. In 1973, she famously won the "Battle of the Sexes" match against Bobby Riggs, and she testified on behalf of Title IX, the federal law that banned sex discrimination in schools. Even so, her outing lost King big-money contracts with corporate sponsors, and it took a long time before she was duly recognized by the athletic community for her considerable accomplishments.

Olympic diver Greg Louganis caused a worldwide gasp when he smacked his head violently against the diving board during an attempted reverse two-and-a-half pike at the 1988 Olympics. It wasn't until 1995, however, that he caused a bigger sensation by telling interviewer Barbara Walters that he had AIDS—and admitted to having been HIV-positive in 1988, when his blood had spilled into the pool.

The difficulty for gays and lesbians to be able to participate in sports inspired a former-Olympian named Dr. Tom Waddell to organize the first Gay Olympics in 1982. More than 1,300 athletes participated that first year in San Francisco. The U.S. Olympic Committee took Waddell to court, trying to bar him from using

TOP: San Francisco held the first Gay Olympic Games in 1982.

BOTTOM: People living with AIDS and their supporters participate in the March on Washington for Lesbian and Gay rights. October 11, 1987.

the word "Olympics" in the name of his event. They eventually won their case in the Supreme Court in 1987, and Waddell had to rename the event "Gay Games." The games are held every four years, and by 2006, the event, held in Chicago, had grown to 11,000 participants.

The Art of the Possible

THE 1980s CONTAINED many setbacks for gays and lesbians, and certainly AIDS was the primary battle to be fought, both at a societal level, and—for too many—a personal one. But there were still enough political gains during the decade to give homosexuals in America hope. One important development was the founding of the Human Rights Campaign (HRC) in 1980 as a gay/lesbian political lobbying organization. By 1988, HRC could brag that it had become the ninth largest political action committee in the country with a budget of $2.1 million. Also, the Gay & Lesbian Alliance Against Defamation (GLAAD) was founded in 1985 to counter inaccurate and sensationalized coverage of the AIDS crisis, and the organization has since developed into a powerful media watchdog group focused on representations of gender identity and sexual orientation.

Activists could also point to some milestone achievements. In 1982, Wisconsin became the first state to pass a law prohibiting discrimination against gays. The next year, lesbian couple Deborah Johnson and Dr. Zandra Rolón successfully tested antidiscrimination legislation in California by suing Papa Choux restaurant for refusing to seat the pair in their "romantic dining" section. Perhaps the biggest political moment for gays and lesbians was the National March on Washington for Lesbian and Gay Rights in 1987. The demonstration drew 650,000 people, making it the largest demonstration for gay rights in history—actually, as historian Lillian Faderman pointed out, at the time it was the "largest civil rights march in American history, far surpassing the 1963 Civil Rights March and the 1969 Vietnam Moratorium demonstration." The march also saw the unveiling of the world's largest artwork: the Names Project's AIDS Memorial Quilt. Originally conceived in 1985 by activist Cleve Jones, participants memorialized loved ones who died of AIDS with a three- by six-foot quilt panel. In 1987, there were almost two thousand panels spread out on the Washington Mall, a sea of grief. Included among the panels were tributes to the flamboyant pianist Liberace and Hollywood hunk Rock Hudson.

The AIDS Memorial Quilt. October 11, 1987.

Then, two days after the march, about eight hundred people (mostly women) were arrested at the U.S. Supreme Court in the largest act of civil disobedience ever held for homosexual rights. They were protesting the *Bowers v. Hardwick* ruling.

As America entered the last decade of the twentieth century, the battle for equality was far from over.

Return of the Queer

AT THE 1990 ANNUAL PRIDE PARADE IN NEW YORK CITY, parade-goers were handed large sheets of newsprint with "I HATE STRAIGHTS!" and "QUEERS READ THIS!" screaming across the top. Then followed an angry manifesto for a new group called Queer Nation, formed in the spring by ACT UP activists to combat homophobia and increase gay, lesbian, bisexual, and transgender visibility. Remember, this was still a time when "queer" was a bad word—no one had used "queer" to mean anything remotely positive for the past fifty, sixty-some years. But times, they were a-changin', and many young gay and lesbian activists felt that they needed to distinguish

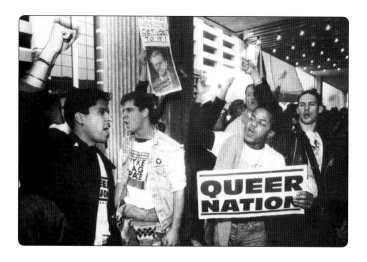

themselves from the previous generation and establish a new, inclusive identity that would better describe the complexity of their gender and sexuality. One Queer Nation member Diane Fagan explained, "I called myself a dyke, rather than a gay woman or a lesbian, because it was a way of separating myself out from the older identity that didn't seem to quite fit." Queer Nation took the antiquated slur of "queer" and reclaimed it as an umbrella term for gays, lesbians, bisexuals, transgendered individuals—anyone, even straight people—who wanted to change the way society forced gender or sexual identities on individuals. The organization spread all over the country within days.

Queer Nation quickly took ACT UP's in-your-face media zap tactics even further, with stunts like the unveiling of a forty-foot banner on the roof of a Greenwich Village bar reading, "Dykes and Fags Bash Back!" The New York group also put together a New Orleans–style funeral procession outside of the Waldorf-Astoria hotel to protest an appearance by President Bush (the father of later President George W. Bush). In Los Angeles, they held phone zaps to overload the office phone lines of antigay politicians and

TOP: Members of Queer Nation hold up protest signs outside of a Jerry Falwell meeting in Houston, Texas. August 19, 1992.

LEFT: Michelangelo Signorile, journalist for *OutWeek* magazine, was an advocate of "outing" closeted homosexual public figures when relevant to a larger story. 1991.

held street protests in 1991 after Governor Pete Wilson vetoed gay civil-rights legislation. In San Francisco, Queer Nation protesters blocked right-wing religious groups from disrupting the massive Halloween party that had become a fixture of the gay community. Two common slogans they used were "Queers Bash Back" and "We're Here. We're Queer. Get Used to It." Indeed, the organization even had plans to organize "Pink Panther" vigilante groups (modeled on the Black Panthers of the civil rights movement) to physically combat homophobic violence. Queer Nation also held protests that weren't just designed for media attention. They wanted to reach Average Joe where Average Joe lived, so they held same-sex kiss-ins at suburban shopping malls and gay marches through predominantly straight neighborhoods.

Dragged Out

ONE CONTROVERSIAL TACTIC SUPPORTED BY QUEER NATION was the "outing" of public figures who were living closeted lives. Activists argued that only by pointing out the presence of homosexuals in every corner of society would homosexuals begin to be taken seriously. In 1990, publishing magnate and multimillionaire Malcolm Forbes died, and journalist Michelangelo Signorile wrote a cover story for a gay magazine called *OutWeek* about Forbes's closeted gay life. Other media outlets were outraged, and a controversy played out over how and when it is appropriate for the press to "out" public figures.

Back in 1975, an assassination attempt on President Gerald Ford was stopped by a Vietnam veteran named Oliver "Bill" Sipple. It wasn't long before the media learned Sipple was gay, and newspapers published that fact. Sipple himself didn't want his family to know about his homosexuality, and when his mother in Detroit read that fact about him in the papers, his relationship with his family became strained. Sipple, already too physically and psychologically disabled from the war to work, fell into a deep depression. He tried suing the newspapers that outed him, but he was unsuccessful. He started gaining weight, ballooning up to about three hundred pounds, and he began drowning his sorrows in booze. On February 2, 1989, Sipple's body was discovered in his apartment—he had already been dead for about two weeks. His tragic story raised important questions about revealing someone's sexual orientation in the press.

However, Signorile maintained that the homosexuality of public figures should be reported when relevant to a larger story. He wrote an *Advocate* article in 1991 publicly outing Assistant Secretary of Defense for Public Affairs Pete Williams. Signorile argued that the hypocrisy of Williams's closeted homosexuality within the top ranks of the Pentagon was newsworthy.

Participants display a banner during the Gay Rights March in Washington, DC. April 25, 1993.

Avenged

AS AN ORGANIZATION, Queer Nation began to wane in late 1992 because of internal arguments over race, gender, and class. Nevertheless, its spirit lived on in a variety of other groups. One of those groups was the Lesbian Avengers, started by six lesbian organizers in the spring of 1992 to fight for lesbian visibility. But unlike the Lesbian Nation movement of the 1970s, these new firebrands weren't interested in separatism—they just wanted to make sure lesbian concerns didn't get lost within a broader queer agenda, and they often worked together with other queer activist groups. By employing camp humor in their direct-action zaps and with slogans like "We are the Lesbian Avengers and We Recruit!" their Queer Nation roots were plainly visible. Cofounder Sarah Schulman dismissed traditional speeches, petitions, and pickets, saying, "These are things that no one ought to have to do again. They are predictable, they don't work, they make people passive."

In 1992, when a local New York City school board rejected a multicultural curriculum that encouraged discussions of homosexuality in schools, the Avengers descended on an Irish Catholic neighborhood in Queens to pass out balloons to kids. Those balloons read, "ASK ABOUT LESBIAN LIVES." When the Promise Keepers—a national Christian men's group that seeks to reestablish traditional gender roles—gathered in Washington, D.C., in 1997, the local chapter of Avengers joined in. Topless. They also distributed parking tickets on cars near the Keepers gathering. The violation? The cars were "Illegally parked in a hate free zone." The penalty was to "Remove your car as soon as possible and EDUCATE YOURSELF!"

There never was any formal organization of the Avengers, as each chapter governed itself and shared only the Lesbian Avengers name and the Lesbian Avenger Handbook. This manual set forth organizing principles that included a ban on theoretical discussions, a rule assigning responsibility for enacting your own ideas, and the requirement of an alternative proposal for any objections to ideas. Avengers spread from New York to Boston, Chicago, and Washington, D.C., as well as internationally to Canada, Britain, France, Germany, and Australia.

Go Forth and Diversify

IT WASN'T JUST LESBIANS WHO WERE CONCERNED about being lost in the broad queer identity—various racial and ethnic groups within the gay and lesbian community began to grow in number and influence during the 1990s. While the National Coalition of Black Gays (later renamed the National Coalition of Black Lesbians and Gays) was started as early as 1978 as the first national organization for black gays and lesbians, other minority groups began to gather and organize throughout the 1980s. The range of organizations included groups of Latinos and Latinas; Asians, South Asians, and Pacific Islanders; as well as American Indians. These groups felt alienated from the queer community not only by white-dominated representations of homosexuality, but also by the same racist attitudes among gays and lesbians that they found in the general population. The differing cultures of America's many racial and ethnic groups meant unique challenges and concerns for their gay and lesbian members—so much so, that it was often hard for "queers of color" to feel they were actually a part of one gay and lesbian community.

But it wasn't just race or ethnic background that brought different groups of queer men and women together in the 1990s. Soon groups were popping up for gay and/or lesbian lawyers, runners, academics, parents, sailors, police, wrestlers, architects, pet owners, computer hackers—you name it, there was probably a group for it. This new diversity of groups was heavily influenced by increased access to the Internet, which fundamentally transformed the way many gays and lesbians were able connect with others like themselves.

AIDS Goes Mainstream

AS THE '90s PROGRESSED, AIDS became seen as more than just a gay issue. Basketball superstar Earvin "Magic" Johnson shocked America when he announced his positive HIV status in 1991—a status acquired through heterosex. The next year, tennis legend Arthur Ashe

announced that he had developed HIV from a 1983 blood transfusion; he died in less than a year's time. By the start of 1995, AIDS had become the leading cause of death for Americans between the ages of twenty-five and forty-four. By the end of the decade, 33 million people were living with HIV/AIDS around the world.

By the early 1990s, ACT UP could point to a number of significant gains. Pressure from the demonstrations forced the government to speed up its drug testing and approval processes. Because of the organization's sophisticated understanding of the medical issues involved with the disease, ACT UP was asked to join many of the medical committees making decisions about the research, as well as helping redesign the clinical trial system. But many of the members died from the disease, and with each political victory, and the hope-filled election of President Bill Clinton, interest and passion in ACT UP dropped off in the middle of the decade.

Real AIDS

IN 1994, MTV'S THIRD SEASON of *The Real World* brought HIV and AIDS into Americans' homes and profoundly affected the way many young people felt about the epidemic. Pedro Zamora was a gay, teenage Cuban immigrant who learned he was infected with HIV while still in high school. Instead of going to college, Zamora became an AIDS educator, traveling to different communities across the country. A friend encouraged Zamora to send in an audition tape to *The Real World* as a way to reach more people about his disease, and after several rounds of interviews, he made it on to the show.

During the five months of taping, Zamora taught his six housemates about his condition, showing them what living with HIV was like and how it was possible to live safely with an HIV-positive person. He even brought some of them along on educational presentations at area high schools. Zamora also fell in love during the season with another AIDS educator, Sean Sasser, and they exchanged vows in a commitment ceremony in the San Francisco loft. Zamora's condition worsened throughout the season, and his new friends even lied to the producers to cover for his illness. Tragically, Zamora died the day after the season finale aired. His memorial service featured a video testimonial in which President Bill Clinton noted that Zamora "enriched and enlightened our nation. He taught all of us that AIDS is a disease with a human face and one that affects every American, indeed, every citizen of the world."

In Bill We Trust

WHEN CLINTON BECAME PRESIDENT in 1993, he seemed to be a godsend to the gay and lesbian community. Queer activists were desperate for a presidential ally after eight years of Reagan and four years of Bush (the first President Bush). In stark contrast, Democratic Party candidate Bill Clinton promised to get rid of the military's prohibition of homosexuals and increase AIDS funding. During the 1992 election, he received 75 percent of the gay vote and $3 million in contributions from the homosexual community.

When he was elected, it seemed like a brand-new day for the advancement of homosexual rights. In 1993, the lesbian and gay community demonstrated its growing strength by drawing nearly a million participants to the Third Lesbian and Gay March on Washington, the largest demonstration in U.S. history up to that point. President Clinton quickly appointed nearly a hundred open lesbians and gay men to his administration. He created the White House Office of National AIDS Policy, then, later, the Presidential Advisory Council on HIV/AIDS. In 1995, Clinton issued an executive order that

TOP: Democratic presidential candidate Bill Clinton stands before a Hollywood backdrop as he delivers an address to gay and lesbian activists during a fund-raising event at a Hollywood nightclub. May 18, 1992.

BOTTOM: Hundreds of thousands of gay rights demonstrators march down Pennsylvania Avenue in downtown Washington, D.C. April 25, 1993.

OPPOSITE: Basketball player Magic Johnson of the Los Angeles Lakers announces his retirement after being diagnosed as HIV-positive. November 7, 1991.

said sexual orientation could not be used as a reason by the government to deny someone security clearances (access to classified information). And when Congress passed a defense appropriations bill in 1996 that would have forced the discharge of any HIV-positive servicemen from the armed forces, the Clinton administration organized a repeal.

Silent Soldiers

A lesbian couple embraces during the Gay Rights March in Washington, D.C. April 25, 1993.

BUT DESPITE ALL THESE ADVANCES, gay and lesbian activists were disappointed by big setbacks during the Clinton years. The first was Clinton's failure to deliver on his promise regarding the military's exclusionary policy toward homosexuals. This policy had been a target of activists for a long time—in fact, one of the earliest homophile picket protests in the 1960s was at the Pentagon for exactly this reason. Then, for the next thirty years, several battles were waged in the courts to try to change the military's discriminatory policy. But in the end, the courts generally supported the military's position. So when the president, or rather, the commander in chief, promised to do away with the policy, activists figured victory was assured.

Not so much. Georgia Senator Sam Nunn set about gathering support in Congress to make the military's ban an actual law, which would prevent the president from changing the regulations. Clinton also encountered significant opposition from the joint chiefs of staff. He eventually caved under the pressure, and in 1993, a compromise policy known as "Don't Ask, Don't Tell, Don't Pursue" became law with his signature—where it remains as of the writing of this book. Homosexual members of the armed forces must keep their sexual orientation a secret, and they definitely can't have sex. Likewise, the military is *supposed to* refrain from conducting gay witch hunts, but when "evidence" is presented about someone's homosexuality, a commanding officer can go to town investigating. Since 1993, more than 11,000 gay and lesbian members of the military have been dismissed under this policy—with a disproportionate number of discharges for women.

Heartbreaker

BUT THAT WASN'T THE END of the gay and lesbian community's disappointment in President Clinton. In 1993, same-sex couples all over the country celebrated when the Supreme Court of Hawaii ruled that the state needed to show a "compelling state interest" in disallowing gays and lesbians from marrying. Could it be? *Homosexuals* might soon be getting *married*? The idea was thrilling because marriage would symbolize how very far lesbians and gays in America had come in the past hundred years, gaining the same rights (and rites) of partnership as heterosexuals. Well over a thousand federal laws and legal policies involve marriage, including Medicare participation, eligibility for first-time home buyer assistance programs, special rules for international adoption, a variety of veterans' benefits, immigration sponsorship qualifications for a partner, as well as all kinds of tax credits. Same-sex couples stood to gain a lot of ground in their fight for equal treatment. While there had been some discussion of legalizing same-sex marriage by activists earlier, it had never been considered realistic enough to be a priority. The Hawaii case turned it into a possibility, and activists realized how beneficial marriage would be in the age of AIDS—not only would committed relationships reduce the amount of HIV transmission, but AIDS had made painfully clear how gay relationships weren't being recognized in issues such as hospital visitation rights and inheritance laws.

However, by 1996, the backlash among right-wing opponents had gathered a lot of momentum. Congress passed the Defense of Marriage Act (DOMA), which restricted federal law from recognizing any unions between two persons who were not a man and a woman, as well as made clear that no state had to accept any other state's definition of marriage.

And President Clinton signed it into law.

Meanwhile, Hawaii argued its "compelling interest" case before a trial judge. In 1996, the judge ruled against the state. But before the appeal was settled, the Hawaii legislature passed a state constitutional amendment banning gay marriage. In 1998, Hawaii voters approved the amendment, and no legal same-sex marriages ever occurred.

But the flickering flame of hope still burned—that same year, a judge in Alaska followed in Hawaii's footsteps by ruling that barring same-sex couples from marriage was a form of sex discrimination (as in, if Jane can marry Dick, why doesn't Harry have the same opportunity as Jane?). Unfortunately, the Alaskan legislature and voting public also followed Hawaii's footsteps, and they amended the state's constitution before any vows were exchanged. Same-sex marriage would have to wait.

Courtship

BUT THE MARRIAGE ISSUE WASN'T THE ONLY REASON gay and lesbian activists found themselves in court during the 1990s, and they began to appreciate how valuable judicial decisions were in protecting and advancing their rights. Back in 1983, Minnesotan Sharon Kowalski had been paralyzed and speech-impaired from a car accident, and her parents were awarded legal guardianship. Kowalski's lover, Karen Thompson, was kept away, even though Kowalski typed out messages of protest. Thompson went to court for guardianship, and finally prevailed in 1991. Though the final ruling gave some legal recognition to a same-sex relationship, the exhausting case was a wake-up call to many gays and lesbians about their legal vulnerabilities.

Then, in 1996, the U.S. Supreme Court struck down a Colorado state constitutional amendment passed in 1993 that prohibited antidiscrimination laws throughout the state from including sexual orientation as a basis for discrimination. As they exhaled a great big sigh of relief, gay and lesbian activists wondered: was the country's highest court reconsidering its antigay views?

Gay Clubbing

IN THE FALL OF 1995, a group of about twenty students wanted to form a Gay-Straight Alliance (GSA) at East High School in Salt Lake City, Utah, as an advocacy group for tolerance and a safe space for queer teens. Unfortunately, the school board got wind of the request and freaked out. They insisted that hosting the GSA would constitute an "endorsement" of homosexuality, and they asked the state attorney general whether they could ban the club. He said no, they couldn't, because of the Federal Equal Access Act from 1984. This law, established by conservative politicians wanting to ensure that Bible study clubs could meet on school property, says that if one noncurricular club can meet, any noncurricular club can meet.

Suddenly, a simple request had morphed into a political storm. The media descended on the school, and Kelli Peterson, at seventeen the oldest of the students, ended up becoming the spokesperson for the group. A few other students talked about starting an *anti*gay club. Then the school board decided to ban *all* extracurricular clubs at local public high schools—and then went about trying to reclassify a number of "noncurricular" clubs as "curricular." Needless to say, many of Peterson's classmates were none too pleased with her determination to stand up for the club.

In 1998, a lawsuit was filed by the East High Gay/ Straight Alliance (with help from Lambda Legal Defense and Education Fund and the ACLU, among other groups) challenging the school board's actions, which the alliance won in 2001—happily, the school had already backed down on its ban on extracurricular clubs and had accepted the East High GSA in 2000.

In 1990 there were only two GSAs, but today more than 2,500 groups are registered with the Gay, Lesbian, and Straight Education Network (GLSEN), the organization that coordinates LGBT History Month (October) and National Day of Silence activities across the nation every year.

On Display

GAY AND LESBIAN VISIBILITY was definitely on an upswing during the 1990s. Several celebrities came out during the decade, including TV journalist Steve Kmetko, author Clive Barker, and fashion designer Yves Saint Laurent, as well as performers such as k.d. lang, Melissa Etheridge, and George Michael. A few athletes came out, too, including ice skater Rudy Galindo, tennis superstar Martina Navratilova, baseball player Billy Bean, and of course Olympic diver Greg Louganis.

In the entertainment world, AIDS stories proliferated and with them, sympathetic portrayals of gay men. On Broadway, Tony Kushner's play *Angels in America* was awarded the Pulitzer Prize in 1993, and the musical *Rent* won Best Musical at the 1996 Tony Awards. Tom Hanks won his first Oscar in 1994 for his performance as a gay man dying of AIDS in *Philadelphia*.

TOP: Kelli Peterson was a founding member of the Gay-Straight Alliance at East High School in Salt Lake City, Utah. April 2006.

BOTTOM: Singer k.d. lang and musician/actress Leisha Hailey (who years later appeared on Showtime's *The L Word*) at an amfAR benefit. 1997.

Actress/comedian Ellen DeGeneres on the cover of *Time*, announcing to the world, "Yep, I'm gay." 1997.

Indeed, the movie industry showed a growing willingness to portray the gay world, notably in *The Birdcage* (1996) and *In and Out* (1997). Also, Rupert Everett's performance in *My Best Friend's Wedding* (1997) cemented the stereotype of a single woman's gay best friend.

Television was getting gayer, too. In 1997, Ellen DeGeneres came out on her television sitcom *Ellen*, sparking a publicity storm that was fueled by her high-profile relationship with actress Anne Heche. Another sitcom featuring gay characters, *Will & Grace*, premiered in 1998 and quickly became a smash success, winning all kinds of awards (including sixteen Emmies) and continuing its run until 2006.

The new queer visibility was alarming to right-wing opponents; in 1999, the Rev. Jerry Falwell hysterically warned the American public that Tinky Winky, a big purple Teletubby, was "damaging to the moral lives of children." (Apparently the character's color, triangular aerial, and handbag were the telltale gay characteristics.) Duly warned, no one cared.

Crimes of Hate

AS THE NEW MILLENNIUM APPROACHED, gays and lesbians all over the country were feeling pretty good about the direction things were heading. Then several high-profile murders reminded them that there was a lot more work to be done.

On October 7, 1998, a twenty-one-year-old University of Wyoming student named Matthew Shepard met two guys at the Fireside Lounge, a gay hangout in Laramie, Wyoming, and asked them for a ride back to campus. The two drove Shepard out to a field, robbed him, severely beat him, tied him to a fence with his own shoelaces, and left him to die. Shepard was discovered eighteen hours later by a passing bicyclist, and he was pronounced dead on October 12. At the trial, the defendants argued a "gay panic" defense: they had gone insane temporarily because they claimed Shepard made sexual advances on them. They also said they had only wanted to rob Shepard, not kill him. The jury was unmoved, and both men received two consecutive life sentences in prison—one could have received the death penalty, but Shepard's family intervened. At Shepard's funeral, a notorious antigay protester named the Rev. Fred Phelps and his family (as members of his Westboro Baptist Church in Topeka, Kansas) carried signs reading "Matthew Shepard Rots in Hell" and "God Hates Fags." Afterward, there was an attempt by President Clinton to add sexual orientation as a protected characteristic to federal hate crime legislation (which would strengthen and expand the Justice Department's ability to prosecute such crimes), as well as a similar move in the Wyoming state legislature. Both attempts failed.

On July 5, 1999, Barry Winchell was brutally beaten to death with a baseball bat by a fellow Army Airborne Division soldier at Fort Campbell, Kentucky, because he was believed to be gay (Winchell was dating a transgender woman at the time). A great deal of publicity followed, with heavy criticism of the ineffectiveness of the "Don't Ask, Don't Tell" policy. It is sad to note that afterward, Fort Campbell significantly increased the amount of gay discharges given out, and reports of harassment in all of the armed services shot up.

If anything good can be said about these sad events, it is that they did not go unnoticed. Shepard's murder inspired a number of songs by celebrity performers, a play titled *The Laramie Project*, and three movies (*The Laramie Project*, *The Matthew Shepard Story*, and *Anatomy of a Hate Crime*), while Winchell's story was told in a Showtime movie in 2003 (*Soldier's Girl*). Transgender youth Brandon Teena had been raped and then murdered a week later on New Year's Eve, 1993, and his death inspired a 1998 documentary and a 1999 feature film, *Boys Don't Cry* (for which Hilary Swank won an Oscar for Best Actress). The portrayals of these horrible deaths reminded Americans that although the antics of Will and Jack might be on TV every week, many American queers lived in terrible danger.

Matthew Shepard. Date unknown.

"It suffices for us to acknowledge that adults may choose to enter upon this relationship in the confines of their homes and their own private lives and still retain their dignity as free persons. When sexuality finds overt expression in intimate conduct with another person, the conduct can be but one element in a personal bond that is more enduring. The liberty protected by the Constitution allows homosexual persons the right to make this choice."

—SUPREME COURT JUSTICE ANTHONY KENNEDY'S MAJORITY OPINION IN *LAWRENCE V. TEXAS*, 2003

6 ⁙ SO CAN WE

2000 & BEYOND

Cambridge, Massachusetts, 2004

"TEN!"

"NINE!"

"EIGHT!"

"SEVEN!"

"SIX!"

"FIVE!"

"FOUR!"

"THREE!!"

"TWO!!"

"ONE!!!"

Front page of *The Boston Globe* celebrating the date marriage licenses were granted to homosexual couples in Cambridge City Hall. May 17, 2004.

It was midnight at last, and the roar of the crowd was deafening. It was the biggest party the city had seen in a long time. Thousands of people crowded Central Square, yelling and clapping, dancing and singing. Some simply watched as all the camera flashes made the stately façade of Cambridge City Hall blink like a strobe light. Bubbles floated along in the springtime air, as if they were being lifted by the music of the brass band below. The crowd bristled with party beads, flowers, and signs such as "See Chicken Little, the sky is not falling" and "Another Southern Girl for Gay Marriage." A chant rippled through the crowd, "We Are Equal"—although at times it sounded more like "We Are Legal."

The entrance doors swung open. Cars passing by on Massachusetts Avenue honked in support. The crowd had already sung "Going to the Chapel," "America the Beautiful," and "This Land Is Your Land." Someone started singing "The Star-Spangled Banner," and rice rained down on the building's steps as the long line of couples slowly crept inside.

It was a good day to get married.

Indeed, the most excited people there were the couples standing in line. There were pierced couples, college students, dyke couples, femme couples, leather-daddies, pregnant women, elderly couples— gays and lesbians of every stripe. Two gray-haired men held a sign stating "49 Years Together!" (their children and grandchildren were pictured on the back). Some of the couples were dressed up in white satin dresses or starched tuxedos, while others wore jeans with their veils, or simply carried a flower.

"I guess this is how straight people feel, to a certain degree," said one ecstatic groom to reporters.

The police SWAT teams that had been assigned to the event formed a double line around the couples to clear their way up to city hall. The protesters, a few members of the Phelps clan from Kansas, had already left. They had only stayed for about fifteen minutes in the roped-off "First Amendment Area," holding their usual signs proclaiming that "God Hates Fags." Perhaps they didn't like that the crowd actually cheered when they arrived. Or perhaps they had seen one of the signs in the crowd: "You're Not in Kansas. Welcome to Equal Rights."

Inside, the city had provided a giant three-tiered wedding cake and champagne. Mayor Michael Sullivan toasted the couples, saying, "May we have those in our arms that we love in our hearts." Marcia Hams and Susan Shepherd had started standing in line the night before—they had been together twenty-seven years, they had a twenty-four-year-old son, and they were the very first to file their applications for a marriage license. (Usually, there was a three-day waiting period, but couples could ask a judge to speed it up and they could return in the morning to solemnize their marriages.)

About ten minutes after midnight, a huge cheer erupted outside when it became clear that the first application had been filed. Every couple stopped at the top of the steps as they left, and looked out at the mass of people cheering them on. Some of them responded by pumping their fists in the air. One man screamed, "Thank you, Massachusetts!" Others simply stood there smiling, enjoying the moment in silence.

A young man in the crowd turned to the older woman standing next to him and asked if she were planning to marry her partner.

She looked at him as if he were nuts. "Us? Oh, we're not getting married. We don't believe in it."

Then she leaned forward and said with a broad grin, "But we've sure as hell been fighting for twenty years to have the right to say no!"

As AMERICA ENTERED THE TWENTY-FIRST CENTURY, the gay and lesbian rights movement made another dramatic shift, this time by focusing its energy toward the fight for marriage equality. The world was changing dramatically, and America faced new challenges such as Al Qaeda's terrorist attacks on New York and Washington, D.C., the epic flooding of New Orleans due to Hurricane Katrina, and the brutal war in Iraq. Same-sex marriage quickly became a lightning-rod issue that polarized politics across the country. Marriage equality activists everywhere continue their battle today, a struggle that has included both significant successes and disappointing failures.

No Camp for You!

IT'S NOT EVERY DAY that an organization like the Boy Scouts of America can make headlines, but the group sure did in mid-2000 when the U.S. Supreme Court ruled in their favor against former Assistant Scout Master James Dale of Matawan, New Jersey. Back in 1990, Dale had been written about in a local newspaper for a speech he gave as copresident of Rutgers University's Lesbian/Gay Alliance. Dale had applied to a leadership position in the Boy Scouts—but not only was he rejected for the promotion, he was booted from the entire organization. Apparently, being gay wasn't acceptable; the scouts explained that their oath requires members to be "morally straight" and that scout law insists they be "clean" in word and deed.

James Dale (right), a gay man who was forced out of the Boy Scouts because of his sexual orientation. June 28, 2000.

Angered, Dale sued. His lawyers argued that the Boy Scouts weren't really a private club, so they were violating New Jersey's antidiscrimination act, which includes sexual orientation. The Supreme Court disagreed, ruling 5 to 4 that the scouts did have a right to decide who can join. Many communities, charities, and corporations around the country responded by stopping their financial contributions and removing the organization's access to public facilities because of the Boy Scouts' discriminatory policy. That in turn led the Boy Scouts organization to stubbornly adopt a written policy reaffirming their exclusion of gays and atheists. North Carolina Senator Jesse Helms even got involved, adding a provision in a federal education act that would withhold funding from schools that denied access to the Boy Scouts.

The Doctor Is Out

FRUSTRATED WITH THE SUPREME COURT RULING, gay and lesbian activists rallied and went right back into battle—this time, against a radio talk-show host and best-selling author named Dr. Laura Schlessinger. ("Dr." of physiology, that is—the study of mechanical, physical, and

ABOVE: Demonstrators protest outside the Austin, Texas, affiliate of CBS, protesting the station's decision to air the Dr. Laura TV talk show. August 26, 2000.

OPPOSITE, LEFT: Father Mychal Judge's official staff photo from the Fire Department of New York. He was the first officially recorded victim of the September 11, 2001, terrorist attacks.

OPPOSITE, RIGHT: Defendants Tyron Garner (left) and John Geddes Lawrence join the celebration at a rally at Houston City Hall celebrating the United States Supreme Court decision that the Texas sodomy law is unconstitutional. June 26, 2003.

biochemical functions of living organisms. Many people wrongly assume that Schlessinger was trained in psychology, which her advice-giving role would suggest.) "Dr. Laura" was the most listened-to radio host in North America in 2000, with about 18 million listeners and with nearly 50,000 callers trying to get through every day. Her show featured Schlessinger's "tough-love" bullying of callers, occasionally offering them such gems of advice as "you're a whore," "he's evil," "they're crappy people," and "they're both sickos." On the topic of gays and lesbians, Schlessinger described them as a "biological error" who "practice deviant sexual behavior." And she *really* got steamed by the idea of gays and lesbians being parents. When she signed a deal with Paramount to put her radio show on TV, her opponents were alarmed. A protest campaign grew around the Web site www.stopdrlaura.com, where site visitors were encouraged to contact advertisers and ask them to disassociate themselves from Schlessinger. A year later, the television show was canceled, and the campaign declared victory.

Heroes

FATHER MYCHAL JUDGE, THE "SAINT OF 9/11," was the first officially recorded victim of the terrorist attacks on the World Trade Center on September 11, 2001. A chaplain of the New York City Fire Department, Judge died inside the lobby of Tower One when Tower Two collapsed. He became an instant national hero: Former President Clinton attended his funeral. Judge's helmet was presented to Pope John Paul II. Congress nominated him for the Presidential Medal of Freedom.

It wasn't long before the press acknowledged the fact that Judge was a gay man. A longtime member of Dignity, Judge had included gay issues as an important part of his ministry. He had

come out to several people in his life, including the fire commissioner, and he proudly marched in the alternative St. Patrick's Day parade in Queens—a parade that pointedly allows gay groups to participate (unlike the country's biggest parade in Manhattan, which has not allowed gay groups to march). A former alcoholic, Judge attended gay Alcoholics Anonymous meetings, and he was widely remembered for his compassionate ministry to people with AIDS.

But Father Judge wasn't the only gay hero to emerge from the tragedy. Mark Bingham was the last passenger to board United Flight 93 at Newark Airport that fateful morning. A large, athletic man (and member of a gay rugby team in San Francisco), Bingham is believed to have been one of the leaders of the passenger revolt that thwarted the hijackers' plans, crashing the plane into the Pennsylvania countryside.

Sex Goes Legal

"**B**OWERS WAS NOT CORRECT WHEN IT WAS DECIDED, is not correct today, and is hereby overruled." With those words, the Supreme Court pulled a 180° reversal of their position on homosexuality just as Pride celebrations were getting started in the summer of 2003. The majority opinion in a case called *Lawrence v. Texas* ruled that sodomy laws were unconstitutional, and for the first time in history, homosexual activity was legal in all of the United States of America. This was huge—so many discriminatory laws on the books were based on the idea that sodomy was outlawed in many states, and those statutes were made immediately vulnerable to legal challenges by this ruling. At last, the *Bowers v. Hardwick* case from 1986 was shelved as an embarrassing episode in the history of the Supreme Court.

ABOVE: Rev. Gene Robinson, Bishop Coadjutor of the Episcopal Diocese of New Hampshire, makes the sign of the cross at the close of the Celebration of Holy Eucharist in Durham, New Hampshire, following his consecration as the first openly gay bishop. November 2, 2003.

OPPOSITE: Actors Heath Ledger (left) and Jake Gyllenhaal in the movie *Brokeback Mountain*. 2005.

Gays in High Places

IN THE FIRST FEW YEARS of the twenty-first century, it seemed that Queer Nation's vision was finally coming true—queer visibility was at an all-time high. Openly homosexual men and women occupied leadership positions as never before. While entertainment figures, such as actress/morning-show host Rosie O'Donnell, continued to out themselves (she spoke up in 2002 to oppose a ban on adoptions by same-sex couples in Florida), there were a few surprises in other fields, as well. In 2003, the Episcopal Church was rocked with controversy when the Rev. Gene Robinson, an openly gay, partnered man, was elected, consecrated, then subsequently installed as bishop of the diocese of New Hampshire. Robinson's new role sparked a major global fight within the Anglican Church, one in which conservative bishops, such as Nigeria's rabidly homophobic Archbishop Peter Akinola, threatened to break with the church. Archbishop of Canterbury Rowan Williams, head of the worldwide Anglican Church, appointed a commission to review the matter, and the panel recommended a statement of regret from the U.S. Episcopal Church. Williams later proposed a two-tier membership to the Anglican Union, with gay-friendly churches having a lesser role in the worldwide union. The issue continues to threaten the church's unity as some bishops in the United States have sided with Archbishop Akinola.

But despite advances in positive gay visibility, some things hadn't changed—homosexuals were still being talked about in the context of scandal, the same way they had been discussed a hundred years before. In August 2004, New Jersey Governor James McGreevey called a press conference to announce that he would resign in three months. The reason? In his words, "My truth is that I am a gay American," and he had been having an extramarital affair with a man whom, it was later revealed, he had appointed as the state's homeland security adviser (with questionably few qualifications). Although McGreevey left office because of the anticipated uproar over the scandal, polls conducted after the revelations showed that statewide support actually went up for the first openly gay governor.

Drama Queers

THERE WAS ALSO A MAJOR RISE IN QUEER VISIBILITY on television programs. The cable network Showtime introduced the American version of the British hit *Queer as Folk* in 2000, a show that followed the (often graphic) lives and loves of a group of gay male friends. The series was an immediate success, continuing until 2005. The network didn't forget about women, either—in 2004, they introduced *The L Word*, a drama about a group of lesbian women. Then HBO aired a star-studded movie version of Tony Kushner's *Angels in America* in 2003, which won numerous accolades and awards. TV networks such as Here! offered strictly queer-interest shows and movies, and soon MTV got into the action, starting its own gay network, LOGO, in 2005. When Bravo debuted a reality show called *Queer Eye for the Straight Guy* in 2003 (in which five gay men give advice to straight men about their appearance, cooking, and home decoration), the show proved to be such a hit that it was picked up by a prime-time network, ABC (Bravo's owner). Although it was widely accepted in the mainstream, the show was controversial within the gay community, where some were bothered by the program's stereotypical premise and portrayals of gay men.

In 2005, those cultural stereotypes were shattered by the movie *Brokeback Mountain*, a tortured love story between two cowboys based on a short story by Annie Proulx. The cowboys were played by two major Hollywood stars, Jake Gyllenhaal and Heath Ledger, and the movie became a fast critical success, raking in more Academy Award nominations than any other film that year. Throughout the summer, newspapers around the country ran related articles on gay men married to women (so-called "Brokeback marriages"), and Brokeback fever soon influenced fashion trends, with cowboy gear appearing in stores everywhere.

Goin' to the Chapel, and We're . . .

Declan Buckly and Kevin Goto kiss after their civil union ceremony in Vermont. June 1, 2000.

AS AMERICANS CELEBRATED the turn of the century in 2000, the idea of same-sex couples marrying legally was considered far-fetched by many, even though Hawaii and Alaska had come close to allowing it in the 1990s. The issue was revived when Vermont introduced civil partnership laws in 2000, which basically permited same-sex couples to marry but called it a "civil union" instead. Then, three years later, the Massachusetts Supreme Court shocked the nation when it ruled that disallowing same-sex marriage was unconstitutional in the state, and the legislature would have 180 days to act, until May 17, before the ruling would go into effect.

But even before that date, San Franciscans stole the spotlight. On February 12, 2004, Mayor Gavin Newsom announced that the city would begin issuing marriage licenses to homosexual couples. This soon led to a whole rash of gleeful marriage celebrations across the country, including Sandoval County, New Mexico; New Paltz, New York; Multnomah County, Oregon; and Asbury Park, New Jersey.

Phyllis Lyon (left) and Del Martin, co-founders of the Daughters of Bilitis, were the first same-sex couple to marry in San Francisco in 2004. The California Supreme Court later invalidated the thousands of same-sex marriages that occurred in San Francisco that year. February 12, 2004.

Then came the backlash. The California Attorney General took the city of San Francisco to court and in March, the California Supreme Court ordered the city to halt giving out marriage licenses to same-sex couples (by then, about 4,000 such marriages had taken place). The San Francisco marriages were soon invalidated, and eventually the rest of the spontaneous weddings would face the same fate. A couple weeks after the San Francisco weddings began, President George W. Bush announced his support for an actual proposed amendment to the U.S. Constitution—called the Federal Marriage Amendment—banning same-sex marriages in all states. Its supporters in Congress tried to force a direct vote on the proposal within months (but failed), and the measure was eventually put to a vote in 2006, when it thankfully failed again.

But nothing could stop the May 17, 2004, marriages in Massachusetts, where thousands of people cheered the couples lining up at Cambridge City Hall. The marriage issue was much discussed in elections a few months later, as eleven states voted on so-called Defense of Marriage Acts. The issue kept coming up in the presidential election that year, although even the Democratic candidate, John Kerry, did not endorse same-sex marriage (though he did support civil unions). For the Republicans, the issue was complicated by the fact that Vice President Dick Cheney's daughter (and campaign manager) Mary was an open lesbian. Candidate Cheney avoided talking about the issue as much as he could, and Mary Cheney later stated that she "actually came very close to quitting" as campaign manager because of the marriage issue . . . but didn't. An organization of gay Republicans called Log Cabin Republicans refused to endorse Bush because of his views on marriage, but it didn't make much of difference: not only was he reelected, but all eleven DOMAs passed in their respective states (Arkansas, Georgia, Kentucky, Michigan, Mississippi, Montana, North Dakota, Ohio, Oklahoma, Oregon, and Utah).

As of the writing of this book, the campaign for legal recognition of same-sex couples continues across the country, with each state a different battleground. Forty-four states have passed "Defense of Marriage" laws, and twenty states have written same-sex marriage bans into their constitutions. The supreme courts in New York and Washington disappointed gay and lesbian activists by refusing to extend marriage as Massachusetts had done. Meanwhile, Connecticut, California, Hawaii, Maine, and New Jersey joined Vermont to offer civil partnerships. California was the first state in which the legislature passed a law instituting same-sex marriage, but Governor Arnold Schwarzenegger terminated—vetoed—it. A case questioning the constitutionality of the federal Defense of Marriage Act is making its way through appeals courts. There are still no final verdicts on marriage cases in the Maryland, Connecticut, and California supreme courts, while in certain states, state legislators have introduced bills making same-sex marriage legal.

Just Married

IN 1892, ALICE MITCHELL WAS REGARDED AS INSANE in part because she suggested that she could marry Freda Ward. Just over a century later, "Boston marriages" no longer refer to the living arrangements of coupled Victorian-era women. They are legal marriages available to same-sex couples throughout Massachusetts today. Marriage is also available to same-sex couples in Canada, South Africa, and several European countries, and even more nations have civil partnership laws. The militaries in countries such as Canada, Great Britain, Sweden, Germany, and Israel accept, indeed *actively recruit*, gays and lesbians. These countries remind us Americans that the fight for equality is far from over, and a brighter, fairer future is within reach.

A quick look back at history inevitably leads us to hope, despite unrelenting discrimination, harrowing hardships, grave losses, and continuing threats to equality. Within one century, homosexuals have gone from being considered depraved sinners, criminals, and sick degenerates to being a political force to be reckoned with, visible leaders in a number of spheres, and proud members of the American public living openly and honestly. No doubt, there's a lot to be proud of.

Bren Bataclan and Robert Parlin wait to apply for a marriage license at the midnight celebration in Cambridge, Massachusetts. May 17, 2004.

NOTES

ABPO   *And the Band Played On* by Randy Shilts
BV   *Becoming Visible* edited by Kevin Jennings
CPO   *Creating a Place for Ourselves* edited by Brett Beemyn
DD   *Different Daughters* by Marcia M. Gallo
DP   *A Desired Past* by Leila J. Rupp
GAH   *Gay American History* by Jonathan Ned Katz
GLA   *Gay/Lesbian Almanac* by Jonathan Ned Katz
GM   *The Gay Metropolis* by Charles Kaiser
GNY   *Gay New York* by George Chauncey
HH   *Hidden from History* edited by Martin Duberman, et al.
IM   *Intimate Matters* by John D'Emilio and Estelle Freedman
MH   *Making History* by Eric Marcus
OG   *Out for Good* by Dudley Clendinen and Adam Nagourney
OGTL   *Odd Girls and Twilight Lovers* by Lillian Faderman
OP   *Out of the Past* by Neil Miller
S   *Stonewall* by Martin Duberman
SPSC   *Sexual Politics, Sexual Communities* by John D'Emilio
SS   *Sapphic Slashers* by Lisa Duggan
TBW   *To Believe in Women* by Lillian Faderman

PART 1: FRIENDS WITH BENEFITS

p. 6 "The 'Love that dare not'" quoted in OP, 49.

p. 8 "I would rather she were dead" quoted in GLA, 225.

pp. 7–9 Fictionalized retelling largely based on Dr. Turner's courtroom testimony, SS, 101–102.

p. 9 "Discussion of the Mitchell-Ward murder" quoted in SS, 42.

p. 9 *term was mentioned neither in court*: SS, 196.

p. 9 *The word "lesbian" was uttered only . . .* SS, 28.

p. 9 *the ancient Greeks left us explicit*: For more on same-sex relations in ancient Greece, and a variety of other cultures and time periods, see *Gay Life and Culture: A World History* (2006).

p. 10 "biological sex is less important": BV, 67.

p. 11 "double vision, with the ability": BV, 70–71.

p. 11 *Usually berdaches were identified before puberty*: OP, 32.

p. 11 For more information on historical records describing the berdache tradition, see GAH, 281–334.

p. 11 "a patriarchal worldview, in which lesbians": HH, 111.

p. 11 "primary personal unit tended to include": HH, 113.

p. 12 *later Americans kept it illegal*: GLA, 44.

p. 12 "Boundaries between romantic friendship": OP, 4.

p. 12 *young Abraham Lincoln and storekeeper*: OP, 4.

p. 13 "adhesiveness" from Whitman's "Not Heaving from My Ribb'd Breast Only" and "Song of the Open Road," the *Calamus* section of *Leaves of Grass*. "Adhesiveness" also was a term used in phrenology, a popular scientific movement that claimed one could read certain personality traits from the shape of one's skull.

p. 13 "the manly love of comrades" from Whitman's "For You O Democracy," the *Calamus* section of *Leaves of Grass*.

p. 13 "For the one I love most" from Whitman's "When I Heard at the Close of the Day," the *Calamus* section of *Leaves of Grass*.

p. 13 "Lew is so good, so affectionate" quoted in OP, 6.

p. 13 "His disposition was different" quoted in OP, 6.

p. 14 *Although at least one historian has pointed out that Victorians*: see Michel Foucault's *History of Sexuality Volume 1*, 17.

p. 14 "When a Vassar girl takes a shine" quoted in OGTL, 19.

p. 14 *For women who graduated college*: TBW, 184.

p. 14 *Though the college graduates, too, would*: TBW, 248.

p. 14 *The pair celebrated the anniversary*: OGTL, 24.

p. 15 *. . . earned her the 1931 Nobel Peace Prize*. More precisely, Addams shared the 1931 Nobel Peace Prize with the president of Columbia University, Nicholas Murray Butler.

p. 15 For more information on the accomplishments of Jane Addams, see TBW, 121–123, or Hull House's Web site: http://wall.aa.uic.edu:62730/artifact/HullHouse.asp.

p. 16 "I feel some inclination to learn whether" quoted in HH, 155.

p. 16 "Susie, will you indeed come" quoted in DP, 44.

p. 17 "my Eve looks into my eyes" quoted in OGTL, 33.

p. 17 "Dearest, It made me quite homesick" quoted in TBW, 132.

p. 17 *Consider that whenever the pair*: OGTL, 25.

p. 17 "You must know, dear, how I long" quoted in TBW, 132.

p. 17 *After Smith's parents died, the two*: TBW, 132.

p. 17 *Whitman kept notebooks in which*: OP, 7.

p. 17 "Depress the adhesive nature" quoted in OP, 9.

p. 17 "To give up absolutely & for good" quoted in OP, 9.

p. 18 "morbid inferences—wh' are disavow'd by" quoted in OP, 12.

p. 18 "The one great difference between you and me" quoted in OP, 12.

p. 18 "accurately describes their committed domestic…" TBW, 1.

p. 18 *Similarly, historian Jonathan Ned Katz has pointed out*: GLA, 19.

p. 19 *Although the word "homosexual" was first used*: GLA, 16.

p. 19 "the most prolific and influential U.S. sexologist": SS, 172.

p. 19 "general mental state is that of the opposite sex" quoted in GLA, 147.

p. 19 "inclinations to both sexes" quoted in GLA, 232.

p. 19 *"inversion" was most commonly used*: OP, 13.

p. 19 "a decided taste and tolerance for cigars" quoted in OP, 19.

p. 19 "modern movement of emancipation" quoted in TBW, 4–5.

p. 20 *he distinguished between "sexual aim"*: GNY, 124.

p. 20 *but many of his followers would argue that*: OP, 25.

p. 20 "nothing to be ashamed of, no vice" quoted in OP, 24.

p. 20 "intensities considerably higher than those" quoted in GAH, 164–165.

p. 21 *becoming commonplace by the close of World War I, when*: OGTL, 35.

p. 21 "too attentive to other women" quoted in HH, 185.

p. 21 *when she discovered she had breast cancer, she tried to treat it herself*: "Murray Hall Fooled Many Shrewd Men," *The New York Times*, January 19, 1901.

p. 21 For more information on "Babe Bean," see HH, 190–192.

p. 23 *In the newspaper's extensive coverage of Wilde's case*, OP, 259.

p. 23 *The* Times *would not print the word "homosexuality"*: GLA, 167.

PART 2: GOOD TIMES . . . & BAD TIMES

p. 24 "You're neither unnatural, nor abominable": *The Well of Loneliness*, Radclyffe Hall. London: Virago Press, 1982, 153.

p. 26 "urged men to leave their wives" quoted in GAH, 391.

pp. 25–26 Fictional retelling based on Gerber's recollection of events, GAH, 390–393.

p. 26 "conduct unbecoming a postal worker" quoted in GAH, 393.

p. 27 *other than an unsuccessful plan by a German immigrant in New York*, DP, 161.

p. 27 *Although in one rare exception, a group of twenty-five*, DP, 123.

p. 27 "Queer wasn't derogatory . . . it just meant you were different" quoted in GNY, 101.

p. 27 "dismiss such ridicule as a sign of lower-class brutishness": GNY, 107.

p. 28 "It was, in fact, bohemian chic for a woman": OGTL, 82.

p. 28 "occasional impulse toward a person" quoted in OGTL, 82.

p. 28 "lived like two bachelors" quoted in OGTL, 87.

p. 29 "To me anarchism was not a mere theory for a distant future" quoted in GAH, 377.

p. 29 *Although Goldman received sexually explicit letters….*: OGTL, 33–34.

p. 30 "prominent feature of these dances [was] the number of male perverts" quoted in GNY, 236.

p. 30 "by the admission of stags and certain mincing undesirables" quoted in GNY, 237.

p. 30 "you would set about hanging policemen from the lamp posts…" quoted in OP, 140.

p. 30 "Greenwich Village, which was once a happy, carefree abode" quoted in OP, 146.

p. 30 *It has been suggested women during the war felt freer*: OGTL, 64.

p. 31–32 *The carefully documented records of the societies' undercover*: GNY, 140.

p. 32 "*Trade*" was a term used to describe: HH, 303.

p. 33 For more information about Eva Kotchover, see GNY, 240.

p. 34 "Paris has always seemed to me the only city" quoted in OGTL, 177.

p. 35 *Sometimes this entertainment was predicated on racist ideas*: GNY, 246–247.

p. 35 For discussion on rent parties and "buffet flats," see OGTL, 74; GNY, 250; HH, 321–323.

p. 35 "spectacles of color" quoted in HH, 324.

p. 35 For more on Gladys Bentley, see OP, 151; OGTL, 72.

p. 35 "rough queers—the kind that fought better" quoted in HH, 324.

p. 36 "funny parties—there were men and women" quoted in OGTL, 76.

p. 36 For more on the affairs of women blues singers in Harlem, see HH, 326, and GNY, 251.

p. 36 "*BD*" stood for "bulldagger," a common term: HH, 320.

p. 37 *According to music historians, a song called "BD's Dream"*: OGTL, 78.

p. 37 "These women, who did not take great pains to pretend": OGTL, 75.

p. 37 *Though no conclusive evidence has been uncovered*: HH, 326.

p. 38 *with one season putting on two hundred and fifty different*: www.musicals101.com.

p. 38 *In contrast, there were only fifty-four shows*: May 31, 2006, press release from the League of American Theatres and Producers, Inc.

p. 38 *At the same time, saucy writer/actress Mae West planned to open*: GNY, 312.

p. 39 *"depicting or dealing with, the subject of sex degeneracy"* quoted in GNY, 352.

p. 39 *"Sex perversion or any inference to it"*: "The Motion Picture Production Code of 1930." Text can be found online at http://www.historymatters.gmu.edu/d/5099/. The Web site quotes *The Dame in the Kimono: Hollywood, Censorship, and the Production Code from the 1920s to the 1960s*, eds., by Leonard J. Jeff and Jerold Simmons (New York: Grove Wiedenfeld, 1990), 283–286.

p. 40 *"Each year saw the production of new novels"*: OGTL, 101.

p. 40 For more information about Jean Malin, see GNY, 317–318.

p. 41 *In 1931, the national RKO chain of theaters even banned*: GNY, 353.

p. 41 *though the biggest of the balls, located in Harlem, would escape*: GNY, 332.

p. 41 *and in 1930s Chicago, semiannual drag*: CPO, 112.

p. 42 *by 1933, the unemployment rate was around 25 percent*: "Compensation from before World War I through the Great Depression," by Robert VanGiezen and Albert E. Schwenk, Bureau of Labor Statistics. Available online at http://www.bls.gov/opub/cwc/cm20030124ar03p1.htm.

p. 42 *"Perhaps the greatest service that you can render"*: OGTL, 96.

p. 42 *Some states even passed laws forcing women to quit*: GNY, 354.

p. 42 *Historian George Chauncey has argued that the loss*: GNY, 353–354.

p. 43 *"there was no question of coming out. I wanted so much"*; "A Very Magical Life: Talking with Samuel Steward," Owen Keehnen, www.glbtq.com.

p. 43 *"very secretive. Everybody was in the closet. There were"* quoted in "A Very Magical Life . . ."

p. 43 *"Gay" had originally meant "care-free"*: GNY, 17.

p. 44 *These men developed a constantly changing system of signals*: GNY, 52.

p. 44 *Known "cruising areas" (places where men . . . encounters)*: For a discussion on Chicago's gay male culture, see David K. Johnson's essay in CPO, 97–118.

p. 44 *"We had to be very careful in those days"* quoted in "A Very Magical Life: Talking with Samuel Steward," Owen Keehnen, www.glbtq.com.

p. 44 *Historian Blanche Wiesen Cook has argued that not only did*: BV, 95.

p. 44 *though the evidence we have left today indicates that Roosevelt's*: OP, 70.

p. 44 *"ER and Hick were not involved in a schoolgirl"*: BV, 97.

p. 44 *her closest friends during the 1920s were two lesbian couples*: OP, 70.

p. 44 *the Franklin D. Roosevelt Library in Hyde Park, New York, has 2,336 letters*: BV, 99.

p. 44 *"sat around an open fire at Lape's Connecticut estate"* quoted in BV, 97.

p. 44 *Likewise, after Hickok's death, her sister destroyed another group of letters*: BV, 96.

p. 45 *"For all the deletions and restraint, the thousands of letters"*: BV, 97.

p. 45 March 7, 1933, letter in BV, 99.

p. 45 March 9, 1933, letter quoted in BV, 100.

p. 45 December 5, 1933, letter quoted in BV, 100.

p. 45 September 1, 1934, letter quoted in BV, 100.

PART 3: LET'S GET TOGETHER

p. 46 *"Persons with homosexual histories are to be found"* quoted in SPSC, 36.

pp. 47–49 Fictionalized retelling based on "Lisa Ben's" interview in MH, 5–15.

p. 49 *"a real sex paradise"* quoted in IM, 260.

p. 50 *"Everybody did it—in numbers."* quoted in GM, 39–40.

p. 50 *"a nationwide 'coming out' experience"*: IM, 289.

p. 50 *"Everybody was released by the war; people were doing"* quoted in GM, 39–40.

p. 50 *"sort of did with their gay behavior what they did"* quoted in GM, 39–40.

p. 50 *"effeminate looks and behavior and by repeating"* quoted in HH, 387.

p. 51 *less than five thousand men were excluded for homosexuality*: GM, 32.

p. 51 *"walked into this office, and here was this man"* quoted in HH, 387.

p. 51 *"mass sexual questioning . . . the first time that they had to think"*: HH, 387.

p. 52 *"worked together in pursuits they could consider"*: OGTL, 122.

p. 52 *the psych exam for women actually favored masculine qualities*: OGTL, 123.

p. 52 *"suddenly you realized the size of homosexuality"* quoted in GM, 37.

p. 52 *"it was really like Alice in Wonderland down the"* quoted in GM, 38.

p. 53 *"sleeping in a foxhole in the desert. . . . We used to call Hitler 'Helen'"* quoted in GM, 36.

p. 53 *"His plane blew up in front of my face"* quoted in HH, 390.

p. 53 *"Punk" was slang for gay men, and black soldiers found guilty*: HH, 389.

p. 53 *"went into a three-day period of hysterics. . . . I was treated with such kindness"* quoted in GM, 34.

p. 53 *If you got a "blue discharge," as they were sometimes called*: HH, 388–389.

pp. 53–54 *From 1941 to 1945, about 9,000 people*: OP, 237.

p. 54 *considering that in the forty years leading up to the war, only a few hundred*: OP, 237.

p. 54 *"I said, 'Well, sir, if the general pleases"* quoted in GM, 47.

p. 54 *In 1944, the Inspector General's office started*: OGTL, 124; HH, 386.

p. 55 *"They started an incredible witch hunt in Tokyo"* quoted in HH, 392.

p. 55 *In the late 1940s, the armed forces discharged about a thousand*: OP, 262.

p. 55 *"The women were all straight, but they knew"* quoted in GM, 51.

p. 56 *some critics even argued that he merely disguised gay characters as straight*: "Suddenly That Summer, Out of the Closet," Randy Gener, *The New York Times*, September 24, 2006.

p. 56 *"helped establish what might be called the"*: "Capote, Truman (1924–1984)," Thomas Dukes, www.glbtq.com.

p. 57 For more information about Kinsey's project, see SPSC, 33–37.

p. 57 *"the work of small boys writing"* quoted in GM, 55.

p. 57 *"Kinsey had implied that the entire"*: GM, 57.

p. 59 *"a corrosive influence upon his fellow"* quoted in OP, 261.

p. 59 *Kinsey's statistics were even quoted and manipulated*: OP, 260.

p. 59 For more on the Crittenden Report, see the Servicemembers Legal Defense Network's (SLDN) Web site, www.sldn.org.

p. 59 For more on the Boise scandal, see MH, 314.

p. 60 For more information on the formation of the Mattachine Society, see SPSC, 59–62.

p. 61 *"masked people, unknown and anonymous"* quoted in "Mattachine Society," Craig Kaczorowski, www.glbtq.com.

p. 61 *years later it was discovered that the FBI had been monitoring*: OP, 341.

p. 61 For more about early Mattachine meetings, see SPSC, 68.

p. 61 *Hay later remembered that even some gay supermarket*: SPSC, 70.

p. 61 *By 1953, the organization had about two thousand members*: SPSC, 71.

p. 62 *The letters to the editor in early issues show that*: SPSC, 72–73.

p. 62 For more about Dr. Evelyn Hooker and Sammy, see MH, 19.

p. 63 *or his book, which went to press seven times*: GM, 125.

p. 63 *"Tolerance is the ugliest word in our language…"* quoted in GM, 128.

p. 63 *"If only all of the inverts, the millions"* quoted in GM, 129.

p. 63 *A Los Angeles columnist wrote an article*: This article appeared in Paul Coates's *Los Angeles Mirror* column on March 12, 1953. SPSC, 76.

p. 64 *Within months, the organization was taken*: MH, 36.

p. 64 *"To be just an organization of upstart gays"* quoted in SPSC, 83.

p. 64 *even Dr. Hooker and Dr. Kinsey encouraged*: SPSC, 84.

p. 64 *"I got lots of complaints about the column"* quoted in MH, 50.

p. 64 *Although in one notable exception, Chicago's black press*: CPO, 119–144.

p. 65 *the first major legal victory for the gay rights*: SPSC, 115.

p. 65 *social roles that started taking shape during the 1940s*: OGTL, 126.

p. 65 *Historians think the roles may have grown out*: SPSC, 99; OGTL, 160.

p. 65 For more about butch-femme culture, see OGTL, 170–172.

p. 66 *butch lesbians in New Orleans knew to wear*: OGTL, 185.

p. 66 *"If you didn't pick a role—butch or femme"* quoted in SPSC, 99.

p. 66 *In the late 1960's, one Springfield, Massachusetts, bar*: OGTL, 169.

p. 67 *in the Canyon Club in Los Angeles, both men and women*: OGTL, 164.

p. 67 For more about alcoholism among working-class lesbians, see OGTL, 163.

p. 67 *Joan Nestle and Judy Grahn have argued that butches weren't*: OGTL, 169.

p. 67 *"would sound like any other women's lodge"* quoted in OP, 338.

p. 68 *"The magazine was called The Ladder because"* quoted in MH, 119.

p. 68 *"[O]ne is oppressed or discriminated against because"* quoted in DD, 22.

p. 68 *"As I quickly learned, the purpose of DOB"* quoted in MH, 111.

pp. 68–69 Mattachine and DOB membership statistics: SPSC, 115.

p. 69 *"Frankly, in the beginning days of the movement, the people"* quoted in MH, 114.

p. 69 *"It's amazing to people now that we put up"* quoted in MH, 116.

p. 70 For more on the Denver branch's demise, see SPSC, 121.

p. 70 *including referrals for discreet doctors to treat sexually*: SPSC, 118.

p. 70 *"I saw the best minds of my generation destroyed"* quoted in OP, 297.

p. 71 *"in this postwar period, they were the first group of American writers"*: GM, 100.

PART 4: BRING IT ON

p. 72 *"What is a lesbian? A lesbian"*: "The Woman Identified Woman," Radicalesbians, 1970 (available online at http://scriptorium.lib.duke.edu/wlm/womid/).

p. 73 For more on the beginnings of CRH, see SPSC, 192–193.

pp. 73–74 Fictionalized retelling based on Nancy May's recollection of events: MH, 139–145.

p. 75 *"It's useless to waste everybody's time"* quoted in SPSC, 194.

p. 76 *"care, discretion, and restraint"* quoted in OP, 342.

p. 76 *Not only that, but newspapers and magazines such as*: SPSC, 138.

p. 77 *even Newsweek and The New York Times ran sympathetic articles*: SPSC, 159.

p. 77 For more on "Randy Wicker"'s visibility efforts, see SPSC, 125, 160.

p. 79 *he had started college when he was only fifteen*: SPSC, 150.

p. 79 For more on Kameny's fight with John Dowdy, see SPSC, 156–157.

p. 79 *"entire homophile movement is going to stand or fall"* quoted in SPSC, 163.

p. 80 Mattachine and DOB membership figures: SPSC, 173.

p. 80 *one city newspaper in 1949 ran the front-page*: CPO, 73.

p. 80 *This population growth was helped by the fact*: DD, xl.

p. 81 *In August 1961, eighty-nine men*: SPSC, 183–184.

p. 81 "*the best known and loved gay man in San Francisco*": SPSC, 188.

p. 82 "*You must realize that the vice squad*" quoted in SPSC, 188.

p. 82 *He got only six thousand votes in the end*: SPSC, 188.

p. 82 *within a year, LCE was printing seven thousand copies*: SPSC, 189.

p. 82 *With almost a thousand members, SIR*: SPSC, 190–191.

p. 83 "*It was thrilling. You knew you were doing*" quoted in MH, 123.

p. 84 "*We had to do the public protests because*" quoted in MH, 134.

p. 84 *homophile groups were popping up all over*: SPSC, 200–201.

p. 84 *In 1966, Mattachine had fifteen branches*: SPSC, 199.

p. 84 *in fact, a mid-1960s study showed that*: OGTL, 192.

p. 86 For more information about the Stonewall bar and the 1969 rebellion, see S, 181–209.

p. 87 "*We are the Stonewall girls*" quoted in S, 201, although Neil Miller pointed out that the *Village Voice* described this performance occurring on Saturday night, OP, 366.

p. 87 "*feminine boys*" quoted in S, 202.

p. 88 "*Screaming queens forming chorus lines and kicking*" quoted in S, 207.

p. 88 "*WE HOMOSEXUALS PLEAD WITH*" quoted in S, 207.

p. 88 "*It's about time we did something*" quoted in S, 208.

p. 88 "*beautiful—they've lost that wounded look*" quoted in S, 208.

p. 89 "*We have got to radicalize*" quoted in S, 211.

p. 89 "*DO YOU THINK HOMOSEXUALS ARE REVOLTING*" quoted in OG, 30.

p. 89 *three to four hundred gays marched to the Stonewall*: OP, 368.

p. 90 "*the black, the feminist, the Spanish-American*" quoted in OP, 371.

p. 90 "*We wanted to end the homophile*" quoted in S, 229.

p. 90 *New York's GLF also sparked the creation of other*: DP, 177.

p. 90 For more on the Barney's Beanery protest, see OG, 33–34, 38–39.

p. 91 "*We were young and idealistic*" quoted in MH, 183–184.

p. 91 "*Homosexuality is a sickness, just as are*" quoted in OP, 373.

p. 91 "*We are no longer willing*" quoted in OP, 375.

p. 91 "*completely and solely dedicated*" quoted in OG, 51.

p. 92 *In 1970, GAA began zapping Mayor*: OG, 54.

p. 92 *though it wouldn't pass until 1986*: OP, 382.

p. 92 *by anywhere from five to twenty thousand*: OP, 383–384.

p. 92 "*This was before SoHo was SoHo…*" quoted in GM, 264.

p. 93 "*complete exchange of energy*" quoted in OG, 56.

p. 93 "*wasn't going to let anybody walk over*" quoted in MH, 240.

p. 93 "*As we walked along, people on the sidewalks*" quoted in MH, 242.

p. 93 "*My mother used to march for me*" quoted in GM, 262–263.

p. 93 For more on PFLAG, see www.pflag.org.

p. 94 Friedan's "*lavender menace*" comments were quoted by *The New York Times Magazine*: DD, 173.

p. 95 "*whenever the label lesbian is used against*" quoted in OG, 90.

p. 95 *two years later, Friedan would tell*: OGTL, 212, although other sources indicate her complaints occurred earlier: OG, 98 and 100.

p. 96 "*For many young women who were*" OGTL, 202.

p. 96 *Many insisted on spelling woman as*: OGTL, 219.

p. 97 *Also, perhaps because lesbian separatist groups were so extreme*: OGTL, 245.

p. 97 "*the closest thing to national personalities*": OG, 71.

p. 97 "*We didn't apply for a marriage license because*" quoted in OG, 57.

p. 97 For more on Jack Baker and J. Michael McConnell, see OG, 56–57, 70–71, 226.

p. 98 *Although in 1975, six Colorado couples*: "San Francisco not the first to marry couples of the same gender," Suzanne Herel, *San Francisco Chronicle*, February 14, 2004.

p. 98 *In 1970, the American Psychiatric Association (APA) included*: OG, 201.

p. 99 *Cheekily called the "Gay PA"*: MH, 254, though it is written as "Gay-PA" in OG, 208.

p. 100 *It wasn't until 1994 that "Dr. Anonymous" revealed*: OG, 208.

p. 100 "*We didn't care. If Jesus could turn water into wine*" quoted in OG, 176.

p. 100 For more on the UpStairs tragedy, see OG, 174–187.

p. 102 "*the general dissipation of the Left, which really*" quoted in MH, 211.

p. 102 *nondiscrimination laws were passed in more than forty*: OP, 401.

p. 103 "*people literally crossed the street not to talk*" quoted in MH, 424.

p. 103 "*the most fabulous disco I'd ever been to in my*" quoted in GM, 292.

p. 104 "*condones immorality and discriminates*" quoted in OG, 297.

p. 105 "*Homosexuals cannot reproduce, so they*" quoted in OG, 304.

p. 105 *she announced plans to open counseling centers*: OGTL, 199.

p. 105 *Similar laws were soon struck down in St. Paul*: OP, 404; GM, 270.

p. 105 *with 250,000 marching in San Francisco alone*: OP, 403, although OG, 319, claims only 200,000 marchers.

p. 106 "*Homosexuals want your children*" quoted in GM, 276.

p. 106 "*Whatever else it is, homosexuality is not a contagious*" quoted in OP, 404.

p. 106 *this became known as the "Twinkie defense"*: OP, 407.

p. 107 *sixty-one police officers and one hundred gays were hospitalized*: OP, 408.

p. 107 *In 1979, activists held the first March on Washington*: BV, 223, though Jennings notes that the federal Park Police estimated that only 75,000 came.

PART 5: SICK & TIRED OF IT

p. 108 "*Our continued existence as gay men upon*": Larry Kramer's "1,112 and Counting" was first published in the *New York Native*, Issue 59, March 14, 1983.

p. 110 *Kramer contacted Dr. Alvin Friedman-Kien, coauthor of*: MH, 425.

p. 110 *Kramer listed twenty-one people whom he had*: ABPO, 245. (Actually, Kramer listed only twenty names, but added that one more friend would be dead by the time the article appeared in print.)

p. 110 *A total of 428 Americans had died*: ABPO, 246.

p. 111 For more discussion on fraudulent responses to the AIDS crisis, see ABPO, 268, 353, 378.

p. 111 *The French had to go so far as to sue the National Cancer*: ABPO, 592.

p. 112 *By then, more than 4,300 people had died*: ABPO, 546.

p. 112 For more information about AIDS, check out avert.org, www.gmhc.org, www.apla.org, and www.aegis.com. For information about the origin of human AIDS, see "Chimp Virus Is Linked to H.I.V." Lawrence K. Altman, published in *The New York Times*, May 26, 2000.

p. 112 *Specifically gay bathhouses had been a fixture*: GNY, 211.

p. 112 *The largest bathhouse in San Francisco, the Bulldog Baths*: ABPO, 23.

p. 113 *In one pre-1980 study of Denver bathhouses, the average*: ABPO, 19.

p. 113 *Hundreds of these establishments across the United States*: ABPO, 19.

p. 113 *Some gay leaders proclaimed that*: ABPO, 391.

p. 113 For more on the bathhouse controversy, see OP, 447, and the time line at www.gmhc.org.

p. 113 "*Oh, God, the battle over whether or not*" quoted in MH, 426.

p. 114 *In 1985, the year all donated blood began*: "Progress in Blood Safety Supply," Monica Revelle, *FDA Consumer Magazine*, May 1995 (available online at www.pueblo.gsa.gov/cic_text/health/blood-ss/blood2.htm).

p. 114 *Today it is less than one in a million*: "HIV and AIDS" at KidsHealth (available online at www.kidshealth.org/kid/health_problems/infection/hiv.html).

p. 114 *By that time, more than six thousand people had been infected*: "Ashe Received a Transfusion Before Blood Supply Was Tested for H.I.V." Lawrence K. Altman, *The New York Times*, April 9, 1992.

p. 114 *Although the CDC had described*: see The GMHC HIV/AIDS time line at www.gmhc.org.

p. 114 For more on President Reagan's silence, see www.gmhc.org, www.aegis.com, www.avert.org, and "The Truth About Reagan and Aids," Michael Bronski, *Z Magazine*, Vol. 17, No. 1, January 2004, and "Reagan's AIDS Legacy Silence Equals Death," Allen White, *San Francisco Chronicle*, June 8, 2004.

p. 114 *Congress had to pass laws to force*: ABPO, 187.

p. 114 "*AIDS is the wrath of God upon homosexuals*" quoted in "Reagan's AIDS Legacy Silence Equals Death," Allen White, *San Francisco Chronicle*, June 8, 2004.

p. 115 "*nature's revenge on gay men*" quoted in *Ibid*.

p. 115 *long after it had been established that HIV could not be transmitted*: www.avert.org. For more on the demonstration, see OG, 558.

p. 115 "*encourage or promote homosexual activity*" quoted in "The Truth About Reagan and Aids," Michael Bronski, *Z Magazine*, Vol. 17, No. 1, January 2004.

p. 115 *Helms also made sure people living with HIV*: www.avert.org.

p. 115 "*Education about AIDS should start at an early*" quoted in GM, 309.

p. 115 *Police in San Francisco were given surgical*: www.avert.org.

p. 115 *There were also reports of landlords evicting*: www.avert.org.

pp. 115–116 "*Such a severe public health concern must cause*" quoted in OGTL, 294.

p. 116 *Polls from 1985 showed that 72 percent of Americans*: the GMHC HIV/AIDS time line at www.gmhc.org.

p. 116 For more on AIDS hysteria, see the GHMC HIV/AIDS time line at www.gmhc.org.

p. 116 "*The disease would convert a generation of*": GM, 284.

p. 116 *In New York, Gay Men's Health Crisis was providing*: www.gmhc.org; ABPO, 282.

p. 116 *The organization started the first AIDS hotline*: www.gmhc.org.

p. 117 *Journalist Randy Shilts calculated that the city*: ABPO, 188.

p. 117 *all despite the fact that statistically they had the lowest*: OGTL, 281.

p. 117 *as historian Lillian Faderman pointed out*: OGTL, 294.

p. 117 *Just before visiting Ronald and Nancy Reagan*: ABPO, 476.

p. 118 For more on Elizabeth Taylor's work on AIDS, see www.amfar.org and "Elizabeth Taylor: Life=Passion," *A&U Magazine*, February 2003.

p. 118 "a tendency ordered toward" from "Letter to the Bishops of the Catholic Church on the Pastoral Care of Homosexual Persons" by the Congregation for the Doctrine of the Faith, available on the Vatican's Web site, www.vatican.va.

p. 118 *Furthermore, the letter ordered church officials to withdraw*: For more information on Dignity, visit www.dignityusa.org.

p. 119 "millennia of moral teaching" quoted in GM, 319.

p. 119 "probably made a mistake" quoted in GM, 320; OG, 539.

p. 119 *Better yet, he thought GMHC should be telling gay men*: ABPO, 167, 210.

p. 120 *When it came out, the drug cost about*: The GMHC HIV/AIDS time line at www.gmhc.org.

p. 121 "You could be dead in less than five years" quoted in OG, 554.

p. 122 "Some of the protesters were taken out" quoted in GM, 323.

p. 122 For more on ACT UP's protests, visit www.actuporalhistory.org.

p. 122 "I want the option of random sex" quoted in OGTL, 256.

p. 122 *Studies during the late 1970s and early 1980s indeed showed*: OP, 468.

p. 122 *several started up lesbian sex businesses in the early 1980s*: OGTL, 254, 258.

p. 123 "women 'play at it' rather than 'being it'" quoted in OGTL, 268. For more on the revival of butch/femme roles, see OGTL, 263–268.

p. 123 *Festival organizers often complied*: OGTL, 251–252.

p. 123 For a discussion on the increasing incidence of motherhood among lesbians during the 1980s, see OGTL, 290–291.

p. 124 "first truly positive portrayal of a gay": "The 80's In Review," *Washington Blade*, December 29, 1989.

p. 124 For more on *An Early Frost*, see Rodney Buxton's article on the film at the Museum of Broadcast Communications' Web site, www.museum.tv.

p. 126 *By 1988 HRC could brag that it had become*: OP, 453.

p. 126 For more on GLAAD, visit www.glaad.org.

p. 126 For more on the Papa Choux case, see MH, 438–453.

p. 127 "largest civil rights march in American history": OGTL, 295.

p. 127 *In 1987, there were almost two thousand panels spread out*: OP, 455.

p. 127 *about eight hundred people (mostly women) were arrested*: www.glbtq.com "Marches on Washington," Brett Genny Beemyn (although Neil Miller counts "some 650" in OP, 457, and *The New York Times* coverage of the protest claimed only six hundred were arrested).

p. 127 *At the 1990 annual Pride parade in New York City*: "Queer Nation," Susan Stryker, www.glbtq.com.

p. 128 "I called myself a dyke, rather than a gay woman" quoted in "When worlds collide: Activists look for life after feminism and ACT UP," Rebecca Lavine, *The Boston Phoenix*, December 1995.

p. 129 *Two common slogans*: "Queers Bash Back" OGTL, 301; "We're Here. We're Queer. Get Used to It," "Queer Nation," Susan Stryker, www.glbtq.com.

p. 129 *Indeed, the organization even had plans to organize "Pink Panther"*: OGTL, 301.

p. 129 For more on Oliver Sipple, see "Caught in Fate's Trajectory, Along with Gerald Ford," Lynne Duke, *The Washington Post*, December 31, 2006.

p. 130 For more on the dissipation of Queer Nation, see Urvashi Vaid's *Virtual Equality: The Mainstreaming of Gay & Lesbian Liberation*, 295–297.

p. 130 "These are things that no one ought to have to do again" quoted in "The NI Interview with Sarah Schulman," Vanessa Baird, *New Internationalist*, No. 267, May 1995 (www.newint.org/issue267/interview.htm).

p. 130 "ASK ABOUT LESBIAN LIVES" quoted in *Ibid*.

p. 130 *When the Promise Keepers—a national Christian men's group that seeks to reestablish*: "Dykes Organize: The Founding of the Lesbian Avengers," Rebecca Roemen (www.gwu.edu/~english/ccsc/roemen.htm).

p. 132 *By the start of 1995, AIDS had become the leading*: www.avert.org.

p. 132 For more information about the success of ACT UP, see "ACT UP," Geoffrey W. Bateman, www.glbtq.com, as well as "We Are Not Crumbs; We Must Not Accept Crumbs," Larry Kramer (available online at http://www.gaycenter.org/events/actupVideo).

p. 132 For more on Pedro Zamora's story, see *Pedro and Me: Friendship, Loss, and What I Learned*, Judd Winick, New York: Henry Holt, 2000.

p. 133 "enriched and enlightened our nation. He taught all of us that AIDS" quoted in *Kaiser Daily HIV/AIDS Report*, part 3, June 6, 2001, available online at www.kaisernetwork.org.

p. 133 *During the 1992 election, he received 75 percent of the gay*: GM, 333–334.

p. 133 *President Clinton quickly appointed nearly a hundred*: GM, 337.

p. 133 *In 1993, the lesbian and gay community demonstrated its growing*: "Marches on Washington," Brett Genny Beemyn, www.glbtq.com.

p. 135 *Since 1993, more than 11,000 gay and lesbian members*: "White House issues first comments re 'don't ask, don't tell,'" *The Advocate*, July 1, 2006 (quotes the Urban Institute, also quoted by U.S. Newswire). For more information on gay and lesbians in the military, see www.sldn.org.

p. 136 *because of the Federal Equal Access Act from*: "Young Activists Fight Intolerance in Utah," Lisa Bennett-Haigney, *National NOW Times*, May 1996 (www.now.org/nnt/05-96/kelliut.html).

p. 137 For more information on GSAs, visit www.glsen.org.

p. 138 "damaging to the moral lives of children" quoted in "Gay Tinky Winky bad for children," BBC News, February 15, 1999 (news.bbc.co.uk/1/hi/entertainment/276677.stm).

p. 139 *Fort Campbell significantly increased the amount*: Servicemembers Legal Defense Network's (SLDN) historical time line of "Don't Ask, Don't Tell, Don't Pursue, Don't Harass" (available at www.sldn.org).

PART 6: SO CAN WE

p. 140 "It suffices for us to acknowledge that adults": Justice Kennedy's opinion can be found at www.law.cornell.edu/supct/html/02-102.ZS.html.

p. 142 "May we have those in our arms" quoted in "Eager couples line up early, gain Massachusetts licenses," Carolyn Lochhead, *San Francisco Chronicle*, May 17, 2004.

pp. 141–142 Fictionalized retelling partly based on "Cambridge plays host to a giant celebration," Joanna Weiss and Lisa Kocian, Globe Staff, *The Boston Globe*, May 17, 2004, and author's interview with David Rosales.

p. 143 For more information about the Boy Scouts' discriminatory policy, see www.scoutingforall.org.

p. 143 For more information about Helms' Boy Scouts Equal Access Act, visit GLSEN's Web site (http://www.glsen.org/cgi-bin/iowa/all/library/record/911.html).

p. 144 "*Dr. Laura*" was the most listened-to: "Talk Radio's Laura Schlessinger: Championing the Christian Right's Social Agenda," Bill Berkowitz, *Z Magazine*, January 2000.

p. 144 "you're a whore" quoted in "Physiologist Laura," Robert Epstein, *Psychology Today*, July 2001.

p. 144 "biological error" and "practice deviant sexual behavior" quoted in "Talk Radio's Laura Schlessinger: Championing the Christian Right's Social Agenda," Bill Berkowitz, *Z Magazine*, January 2000.

p. 144 *And she really got steamed by the idea*: Ibid.

p. 144 For more on the Schlessinger protests, visit www.stopdrlaura.com.

p. 144 For more on Father Mychal Judge, see "The Firemen's Friar," Jennifer Senior, *New York Magazine*, November 12, 2001 (nymag.com/nymetro/news/sept11/features/5372/).

p. 144 *A longtime member of Dignity, Judge had included gay issues*: "A Love Supreme: The Fallen Fire Chaplain Was Also a Hero to Gays," Andy Humm, *Village Voice*, October 1, 2001.

p. 145 "*Bowers* was not correct when it was decided, is not": the *Lawrence v. Texas* ruling can be read online at http://www.law.cornell.edu/supct/html/02-102.ZS.html.

p. 147 *polls conducted after the revelations showed*: "Majority in New Jersey Support Gay Marriage," Beth Shapiro, www.365gay.com, posted May 4, 2005. Shapiro refers to a Zogby International poll conducted for Garden State Equality. "Poll: NJ Governor's Approval Nudges Up," Associated Press, *USA Today*, posted August 15, 2004. The article refers to a *Star-Ledger*/Eagleton-Rutgers poll.

p. 148 For more information about the fight for marriage equality, visit www.hrc.org.

p. 149 "actually came very close to quitting": *David Letterman Show*, May 19, 2006.

SELECTED BIBLIOGRAPHY

Aldrich, Robert, ed. *Gay Life and Culture: A World History.* London: Thames & Hudson, 2006.

Beemyn, Brett, ed. *Creating a Place for Ourselves: Lesbian, Gay, and Bisexual Community Histories.* New York: Routledge, 1997.

Chauncey, George. *Gay New York: Gender, Urban Culture, and the Making of the Gay World, 1890–1940.* New York: Basic, 1994.

Clendinen, Dudley, and Adam Nagourney. *Out for Good: The Struggle to Build a Gay Rights Movement in America.* New York: Touchstone, 1999.

Deitcher, David. *Dear Friends: American Photographs of Men Together, 1840–1918.* New York: Abrams, 2001.

D'Emilio, John. *Sexual Politics, Sexual Communities: The Making of a Homosexual Minority in the United States, 1940–1970.* 2nd ed. Chicago: University of Chicago, 1998.

D'Emilio, John, and Estelle B. Freedman. *Intimate Matters: A History of Sexuality in America.* 2nd ed. Chicago: University of Chicago: 1997.

Duberman, Martin. *Stonewall.* New York: Dutton, 1993; reprint, New York: Plume, 1994. (Page citations are to the reprint edition.)

Duberman, Martin, Martha Vincinus, and George Chauncey, Jr, eds. *Hidden from History: Reclaiming the Gay and Lesbian Past.* 2nd ed. New York: Meridian, 1989.

Duggan, Lisa. *Sapphic Slashers: Sex, Violence, and American Modernity.* Durham, N.C.: Duke University Press, 2000.

Faderman, Lillian. *Odd Girls and Twilight Lovers: A History of Lesbian Life in Twentieth-Century America.* New York: Penguin, 1991.

———. *To Believe in Women: What Lesbians Have Done for America—A History.* New York: Mariner, 2000. (First published 1999)

Foucault, Michel. *The History of Sexuality: Volume I: An Introduction,* trans. Robert Hurley; originally published as *La volonté de savoir* (Paris: Editions Gallimard, 1976). New York: Random House, 1978; reprint, New York: Vintage, 1990. (Page citations are to the reprint edition.)

Gallo, Marcia. *Different Daughters: A History of the Daughters of Bilitis and the Rise of the Lesbian Rights Movement.* New York: Carroll & Graf, 2006.

Jennings, Kevin, ed. *Becoming Visible: A Reader in Gay and Lesbian History for High School and College Students.* Boston: Alyson, 1994.

Kaiser, Charles. *The Gay Metropolis: 1940–1996.* New York: Harvest, 1997.

Katz, Jonathan Ned. *Gay American History: Lesbians and Gay Men in the U.S.A.* Revised ed. New York: Meridian, 1992.

———. *Gay/Lesbian Almanac: A New Documentary.* New York: Carroll & Graf, 1994; reprint, New York: Harper & Row, 1983. (Page citations are to the reprint edition.)

Marcus, Eric. *Making History: The Struggle for Gay and Lesbian Equal Rights, 1945–1990: An Oral History.* New York: HarperCollins, 1992.

Miller, Neil. *Out of the Past: Gay and Lesbian History from 1869 to the Present.* New York: Vintage, 1995.

Rupp, Leila J. *A Desired Past: A Short History of Same-Sex Love in America.* Chicago: University of Chicago Press, 1999.

Shilts, Randy. *And the Band Played On: Politics, People, and the AIDS Epidemic.* New York: St. Martin's, 1988.

Vaid, Urvashi. *Virtual Equality: The Mainstreaming of Gay and Lesbian Liberation.* New York: Anchor, 1996.

Winick, Judd. *Pedro and Me: Friendship, Loss, and What I Learned.* New York: Holt, 2000.

ILLUSTRATION CREDITS

Cover: © Getty Images; **Title page:** © Owen Franken/CORBIS; **p. 4:** Courtesy of Maria Middleton; **p. 8:** Courtesy of *The New York Times*; **p. 11:** © National Anthropological Archives, Smithsonian Institution; **p. 12:** Photographer Unknown. Courtesy of Herbert Mitchell; **p. 13:** Unidentified Photographer, [Two Unidentified Men], ca. 1860, Ambrotype, International Center of Photography, Gift of Brain Wallis in honor of David Deitcher and Clayton Guthrie, 2001; **p. 15:** Courtesy of the Jane Addams Collection, Swarthmore College Peace Collection; **p. 16:** © CORBIS; **p. 18:** © CORBIS; **p. 19:** © Hulton-Deutsch Collection/CORBIS; **p. 20:** © Bettmann/CORBIS; **p. 21:** Drawing from the Stockton *Evening Mail,* October 9, 1897; **p. 22:** © Roger Viollet Collection/Getty Images; **p. 23:** From the *American Journal of Urology and Sexology* 13 [1917]: 455; **p. 28:** From *Broadway Brevities,* June 6, 1932; **p. 29** (top): © Underwood & Underwood/CORBIS; **p. 29** (bottom): © Bettmann/CORBIS; **p. 31:** © Bettmann/CORBIS; **p. 33:** © Hulton Archive/Getty Images; **p. 34** (top): © Paul Thompson/FPG/Getty Images; **p. 34** (bottom): © Bettmann/CORBIS; **p. 35:** © Underwood & Underwood/CORBIS; **p. 36:** © Underwood & Underwood/CORBIS; **p. 37** (top): © Frank Driggs Collection/Getty Images; **p. 37** (bottom): © MPI/Getty Images; **p. 38:** © Bettmann/CORBIS; **p. 39:** © Condé Nast Archive/CORBIS; **p. 40** (top): © Fox Photos/Getty Images; **p. 40** (bottom): From *Vanity Fair,* February 1931. Courtesy of *Vanity Fair* © 1931 [renewed 1959] by Condé Nast Publications, Inc.; **p. 42:** © CORBIS; **p. 43:** Courtesy of the Navy Art Collection; **p. 45:** © Bettmann/CORBIS; **p. 48:** Courtesy of Lisa Ben; **p. 50:** © Esther Bubley/Getty Images; **p. 51:** © Swim Ink 2, LLC/CORBIS; **p. 52:** © Swim Ink 2, LLC/CORBIS; **p. 54:** Courtesy of Johnnie Phelps; **p. 55:** Courtesy of Pocket Books; **p. 56** (top): © Bettmann/CORBIS; **p. 56** (bottom): © Bettmann/CORBIS; **p. 57:** © Wallace Kirkland/Time Life Pictures/Getty Images; **p. 58:** © RKO Pictures/Getty Images; **p. 59:** © Hank Walker/Time Life Pictures/Getty Images; **p. 60** © John Gruber; **p. 62** (top): Courtesy of the ONE National Gay & Lesbian Archives; **p. 62** (bottom): © Karl Muenzinger; **p. 63:** Courtesy of Ayer Company Publisher; **p. 65:** Courtesy of Frankie Hucklenbroich; **p. 66:** Courtesy of Betty Jetter; **p. 68:** Courtesy of Phyllis Lyon; **p. 69:** © Bettmann/CORBIS; **p. 71** (top): © Allen Ginsberg/CORBIS; **p. 71** (bottom): © Allen Ginsberg/CORBIS; **p. 74:** Courtesy of the *San Francisco Chronicle*; **p. 76:** © Bettmann/CORBIS; **p. 77:** Courtesy of the GLBT Archives of Philadelphia; **p. 78** (top): © Grey Villet/Time Life Pictures/Getty Images; **p. 78** (bottom): Courtesy of I.G.I.C. Collection; **p. 81:** Courtesy of the GLBT Historical Society; **p. 82:** Courtesy of Herbert Donaldson; **p. 83:** © Bettmann/CORBIS; **p. 85:** © Bettmann/CORBIS; **p. 86:** Public domain; **p. 88:** Photo by Peter Hujar; **p. 90:** Courtesy of the William Canfield papers, Northeastern University Archives; **p. 92** (top): Richard C. Wandel, LGBT Community Center, National Archive of Lesbian and Gay History; **p. 92** (bottom): JP Laffont/Sygma/CORBIS; **p. 93:** UPI/Bettmann News Photos; **p. 94** (top): Reproduced with permission of PFLAG National; **p. 94** (bottom): © Bettmann/CORBIS; **p. 95:** © JP Laffont/Sygma/CORBIS; **p. 96:** Courtesy of Cathy Cade; **p. 98:** © Grey Villet/Time Life Pictures/Getty Image; **p. 99:** Star Collection, reprinted by permission of the DC Public Library © Washington Post; **p. 100:** © Kay Tobin Lahusen; **p. 101:** © JP Laffont/Sygma/Corbis; **p. 102:** © Bernard Gotfryd/Getty Images; **p. 103:** © Robin Platzer/Twin Images & Online USA/Getty Images; **p. 104:** © CBS Archive/Getty Images; **p. 105** (right): © Bettmann/CORBIS; **p. 105** (left): © Roger Ressmeyer/CORBIS; **p. 106:** © Bettmann/CORBIS; **p. 107:** © Roger Ressmeyer/CORBIS; **p. 109:** Courtesy of Charles Ortleb, *New York Native*; **p. 110:** © Sara Krulwich/New York Times Co./Getty Images; **p. 111:** © Bettmann/CORBIS; **p. 112:** © Bettmann/CORBIS; **p. 113:** © Yvonne Hemsey/Getty Images; **p. 114:** © Bettmann/CORBIS; **p. 115:** © Bettmann/CORBIS; **p. 117:** © Getty Images; **p. 118:** © Terry Ashe/Time Life Pictures/Getty Images; **p. 119:** © Bettmann/CORBIS; **p. 120** (top): Courtesy of ACT UP; **p. 120** (bottom): © DAVID A. CATOR/AFP/Getty Images; **p. 121:** © Viviane Moos/CORBIS; **p. 122:** © Roger Ressmeyer/CORBIS; **p. 123:** © John Springer Collection/CORBIS; **p. 124** (top): © Bernard Gotfryd/Getty Images; **p. 124** (bottom): © Focus on Sport/Getty Images; **p. 125:** © BRIAN SMITH/AFP/Getty Images; **p. 126** (top): © JP Laffont/Sygma/Corbis; **p. 126** (bottom): © Bettmann/CORBIS; **p. 127:** © Jean Louis Atlan/Sygma/Corbis; **p. 128** (top): © Najlah Feanny/CORBIS SABA; **p. 128** (bottom): © Jodi Buren/Time & Life Pictures/Getty Images; **p. 130:** © Porter Gifford/Liaison/Getty Images; **p. 132:** © Stephen Dunn/Getty Images; **p. 133** (top): © MIKE NELSON/AFP/Getty Images; **p. 133** (bottom): © PAUL RICHARDS/AFP/Getty Images; **p. 134:** © Porter Gifford/Liaison/Getty Images; **p. 137** (top): Courtesy of Don Romesburg; **p. 137** (bottom): © Marion Curtis/DMI/Time Life Pictures/Getty Images; **p. 138:** © Time Inc./Time Life Pictures/Getty Images; **p. 139:** © CORBIS SYGMA; **p. 141:** Courtesy of the *Boston Globe*; **p. 143:** © NORCIA MICHAEL/NY POST/CORBIS SYGMA; **p. 144:** © BIRCHUM JANA/CORBIS SYGMA; **p. 145** (left): Public domain; **p. 145** (right): © Erich Schlegel/Dallas Morning News/Corbis; **p. 146:** © Michael Springer/Getty Images; **p. 147:** © epa/Corbis; **p. 148:** © FRI/CORBIS SYGMA; **p. 149:** © Liz Mangelsdorf/San Francisco Chronicle/Corbis; **p. 151:** Courtesy of the San Francisco Chronicle. Chronicle photo by Deanne Fitzmaurice.

INDEX